Cracking Codes

The Knowledge

Cracking Codes

Diana Kimpton

Illustrated by
Mike Phillips

Hippo

For Matt and Tom

Scholastic Children's Books,
Euston House, 24 Eversholt Street,
London NW1 1DB, UK
A division of Scholastic Ltd
London ~ New York ~ Toronto ~ Sydney ~ Auckland
Mexico City ~ New Delhi ~ Hong Kong

Published in the UK by Scholastic Ltd, 2003

Text copyright © Diana Kimpton, 2003
Illustrations copyright © Mike Phillips, 2003

10 digit ISBN 0 439 98184 0
13 digit ISBN 978 0439 98184 2

All rights reserved
Typeset by Falcon Oast Graphic Art Ltd
Printed and bound by Nørhaven Paperback A/S, Denmark

6 8 10 9 7

Contents

Introduction

How good are you at keeping secrets? I hope you're brilliant because you are about to learn loads of them. Codes are brilliant at keeping secrets, too, and secrets are always fascinating.

But wherever there is a secret, there is always someone trying to find out what it is. So as soon as the codemakers dream up a new code, the codebreakers set to work trying to crack it.

That's why there is a constant battle between the codemakers and the codebreakers – a battle that's shaped history, won wars and cost one very important person her head.

While that battle has raged on, codes have been used by soldiers, spies, lovers, smugglers, gamblers and kings. They've kept diaries safe from prying eyes, prevented magic spells falling into the wrong hands and helped generations of children pass secret messages in class.

Now you have the chance to enter the secret world of codes yourself. Shhh. Don't tell a soul. Put on your dark glasses and a false moustache. Find a quiet corner where no one is watching and read on. In the process you'll learn how codes work, how to crack them and how to read minds. With any luck, you'll also put a stop to a criminal mastermind's dastardly plot.

But remember. If anyone looks over your shoulder, shut the book quickly and say,

Shhh. It's a secret.

Code-Cracking Timeline

1500 BC

An ancient potter uses code to hide his secret recipe for pottery glaze and becomes the first codemaker ever (or at least the first one anyone knows about).

6th century BC

An Egyptian graffiti artist writes "I, Victor, the humble poor man – remember me" in code on a monastery wall ... and we do, now we've cracked his code. But no one knows why he chose to use one in the first place.

5th century BC

The Spartans use a gadget called a scytale to hide their secret messages from prying eyes.

8th–9th centuries AD

The Arabs invent cryptanalysis – the art of cracking codes. And about time too – the codemakers have had everything their own way for over 2,000 years.

Late 15th century

Arnaldus de Bruxella uses code to hide his recipe for making a philosopher's stone which was supposed to turn ordinary metals into gold. But he doesn't mention Harry Potter.

1587

Mary Queen of Scots wrongly thinks her code is uncrackable. She finds out the hard way that it's not and pays for her mistake with her life.

Late 17th century

Antoine Rossignol and his son invent the Great Cipher of Louis XIV which is not cracked for another 200 years.

18th century

Vienna becomes famous for the skill of the codebreaking team working in its Black Chamber.

1812

Napoleon's invasion of Russia fails thanks to the bitter Russian winter and the work of the Russian codebreakers.

1844

The newly invented telegraph uses Morse Code to send messages quickly. The resulting lack of privacy encourages ordinary people to use codes.

1876

Telegrams in code are used to try to fix the result of the US presidential election. The telegrams are cracked in 1878 after they are published in newspapers.

1885

The publication of the Beale Ciphers triggers a hunt for hidden treasure.

1914–1918

Sending messages by radio during the First World War makes them easier to intercept so codes become more important. It also helps the codebreakers by giving them huge numbers of coded messages to study.

1917

A decoded telegram leads to the USA entering the First World War.

1928

President Hoover's Secretary of State closes the USA's Black Chamber because "gentlemen should not read each other's mail".

1933

"Rumrunners" smuggling illegal alcohol into the USA are caught after their coded messages are cracked.

1939–1945

The cracking of the Enigma code machine helps the Allies win the Second World War.

1948

Norman Woodland and Bernard Silver invent barcodes before the technology exists to use them.

1957

Russian agent Colonel Abel discovers a big snag with "one-time pads" – being found with one helps prove he's a spy.

1960s and 70s

The growing use of computers increases demand for codes to hide the information they contain.

1994

Aldrich Ames, a Russian spy working inside the CIA, is caught after American agents crack the password protection on his computer and decode his files.

Today

Everyone uses codes all the time. Computer codes keep your information safe when you shop online and barcodes help you whizz through the checkout at the supermarket. At the same time, governments, spies and criminals continue to use them for secret messages.

The Secret World of Codes

The world of codes is shrouded in secrecy. It's also full of subterfuge, misinformation and downright lies. But there is a very good reason for this sneaky behaviour.

Once you've cracked a code, you can read all the other messages that are sent using it. But as soon as your opponents discover what you've done, they will switch to a new code and you will be back to square one. So sensible codebreakers have always kept very quiet about their successes in the hope of lulling the codemakers into a false sense of security.

Secrecy and the Black Chambers

Black Chambers weren't very dirty bedrooms or a dark solution to the lack of medieval toilets. They were teams of codebreakers used by European governments from the sixteenth century onwards.

Each government allowed all the others to send diplomats to live in their country. But the governments didn't trust each other so they secretly intercepted all the diplomats' letters and read them before sending them on to their final destination.

HANG ON A MINUTE, IF WE'RE READING THEIR LETTERS, THEY'RE PROBABLY READING OURS!

Because they guessed what was happening, the diplomats wrote in code. That's where the code-cracking skills of the Black Chambers came in useful.

In the eighteenth century, Vienna's Black Chamber was believed to be the best in Europe. It worked like this.

A diplomat wrote a letter, closed it with a blob of wax and pressed his government's seal into the warm wax to make an easily recognizable mark. The sealing wax was supposed to stop anyone reading it secretly (some hope!).

SQUELCH!

The letter was intercepted and taken to the Black Chamber, where the sealing wax was carefully melted with a candle.

OOPS!

The letter was copied by hand – there were no photographs or photocopiers in those days.

I WISH THERE WAS A QUICKER WAY OF DOING THIS!

The copy went to the codebreakers to be cracked.

WHICH ONE'S THE COPY?

The original letter was resealed with matching sealing wax marked with a copy of the original seal.

NOT THAT KIND OF SEAL, STUPID!

The codebreakers were so crucial to the success of the Black Chambers that they were paid extra bonuses if they cracked an important code. As a result, the best codebreakers became rich and important, much to the surprise of ordinary people who hadn't a clue what they did.

The Restoration Review 1660

SHOCK NEWS FROM PALACE

Surprise greeted news that John Wallis is working for King Charles II. Wallis worked against Charles' dad, King Charles I, throughout the Civil War. His exact role in the conflict remains shrouded in secrecy but reliable rumours suggest sneaky Wallis played a significant part in the downfall of Charles I, who ended up losing his head 11 years ago!

Our roving reporter asked the palace why our new king is happy to employ someone who worked against his poor old dad, and why he pays megabucks to a man who switched sides so easily?

A Palace spokesman replied, "Go away before I empty this black chamber pot over your head."

What that reporter didn't know was that John Wallis was the Parliamentarians' top codebreaker. Charles II needed his skills so much that he was willing to overlook the past.

Leaky Chambers

Sometimes the secrecy surrounding the Black Chambers wasn't good enough to prevent leaks. In 1774, a masked man sold a bundle of papers to the French which contained all the messages recently decoded in Vienna.

The French thought it was a great deal – it saved them hours of work.

The Great Cipher

France's real claim to fame in the secret world of codes is the Great Cipher of Louis XIV. It was created during the second half of the seventeenth century and was so cunningly designed that no one cracked it for more than 200 years.

The champion codebreaker who finally unlocked the secrets of the Great Cipher was called Étienne Bazeries. He started work on it in 1890 and, after months of work and many false starts, he finally discovered how it worked. Some of its 587 different numbers stood for letters, some for syllables, and one particularly fiendish one told the person decoding the message to ignore the previous number.

One of the secret messages he decoded was about a mysterious prisoner who was only allowed out of his cell wearing a mask. No one knew who he was but there were many rumours about his identity.

I RECKON HE'S THE SECRET TWIN BROTHER OF THE KING, LOCKED AWAY SO HE CAN'T CLAIM THE THRONE.

I THINK I'LL WRITE A BOOK ABOUT THIS.

DUMAS

The secret letter said the prisoner was someone called General Bulonde. That was a real disappointment. It was nowhere near as exciting as the rumours or the book, *The Man in the Iron Mask*, written by Alexandre Dumas. The mystery was solved – or was it? When it comes to keeping secrets, codebreakers and kings will go to great lengths to hide the truth. What do you think?

The Zimmerman telegram

Sometimes codebreakers and governments face a dilemma when their code-cracking successes reveal a really momentous secret. They need to use the information they've discovered but if they do they know that they'll give away the fact that they have cracked the code. That's what happened at the beginning of 1917 when the British intercepted a telegram in code.

By then, the First World War had been raging for more than two years. The opposing armies faced each other in the trenches where thousands of men died in battles which only moved the front line a few metres forwards or backwards. Many countries had been drawn into the war but the USA remained uninvolved.

As the British codebreakers worked on the telegram, they quickly realized how important it was.

Top Secret Report

Subject – telegram dated 16 January 1917

Sent by Arthur Zimmerman, German Foreign Minister
Sent to German ambassador, Washington
Code – 0075

This telegram reveals German plans to encourage Mexico to attack the USA and reconquer Texas, New Mexico and Arizona.

The good news is that, if we show it to the USA, it will probably bring them into the war and we could do with their help.

The bad news is that the Germans will then realize we've cracked code 0075 and change to one we don't know. This would be a disaster – it's taken us months to crack 0075.

After some head-scratching, the British had a brainwave. They realized that the Germans had probably sent the same information to their ambassador in Mexico. They also knew that particular ambassador never used code 0075, so they guessed his telegram might have been sent using a different one. To check this, they sent a secret agent to steal a copy of the Mexican telegram.

To their delight, they were right. The new telegram was in a much less fiendish code than 0075 and the British didn't mind the Germans knowing they'd cracked that one. It was also slightly different from the one to Washington so the Germans would be able to recognize which telegram they leaked.

The British kept very quiet about the Washington telegram but secretly gave the Mexican one to the US government. They, in turn, released it to the papers and everyone was shocked to learn the Germans' plans. Eventually the news led to America joining the war against Germany – a decision that helped bring the war to an end.

Although the Zimmerman telegram changed the course of history, it didn't break the secrecy surrounding the British codebreakers. The Germans thought that only the Mexican version of the telegram had been read so they never realized code 0075 had been cracked.

Which just goes to show that you can never rely on anything in the secret world of codes. Even the jargon can be confusing, so, before we go any further, let's look at what some of it means.

Codes or Ciphers?

If you want to crack codes, you need to know that there are two different kinds of secret writing: *codes*, which replace whole words with other words or groups of letters, and *ciphers*, which replace individual letters or sounds with symbols or change the order of the letters.

Although codes and ciphers are different, the word code is often used in a general way to mean any kind of secret writing. Confusing, isn't it?

This is a good moment to introduce you to Luke Warm, secret agent W7. He needs to send you this message.

He doesn't want anyone else to know where you are meeting so he needs to disguise the information in some way.

He could use a code to replace "cinema" with a different word.

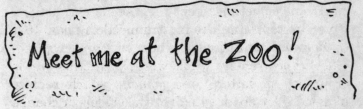

Meet me at the zoo!

Or he could use a cipher to replace each letter in "cinema" with the next one in the alphabet.

Meet me at the djofnb!

Of course, neither system is any use unless you know how to work out what it means.

Luke has only used his code or cipher to disguise the most important word in the message. The rest of it is not disguised at all – in code jargon, it is "in clear".

He's not the first person to use this technique. It's been around for over 2,000 years. Ancient magicians sometimes kept their spells and potions secret by replacing the most important facts with codewords or disguising them with cipher.

My Spiffing Spell:
by
Wizard Swingle the
Sweet-toothed

Crush one dried bat.
Blend with half a litre of dragon's blood.
Mix in two eyes of lizard.
Add one frog.

That sounds disgusting, doesn't it? But you may think differently if you know his code.

Dried bat = banana; Dragon's blood = milk; Eye = teaspoon; Lizard = sugar; Frog = cherry

Sending your reports

All your reports are TOP SECRET. Do NOT send them in clear.

First write your report in ordinary language. This is the *plaintext* version.

Now use your code or cipher to hide your report. This process is called *encoding*, *enciphering* or *encryption*.

You now have a disguised version of your report – the *codetext* or *ciphertext*.

Send this to headquarters.

We will turn your report back into the plaintext version. This process is called *decoding*, *deciphering* or *decryption*.

PLEASE NOTE It is traditional to write the plaintext in small (or lower case) letters and the ciphertext in capital letters.

Codes without writing

All the codes we've met so far have been written down. But writing isn't the only way of communicating and it's not the only way of using codes.

Fires

A large fire on top of a hill makes a good signal because it's visible for miles around, especially at night. In 1588, the Elizabethans knew the Spanish were planning to attack so they built a series of fires called beacons along the coast of England and

Wales and inland to London. The first people to see the ships lit their fire. When the next people along the coast saw the first fire, they lit theirs, and so on all the way to London. The code was pretty simple:

Hands

Waving your arms is a natural way of signalling but they are hard to see from a distance. You can make them more visible by holding a flag in each hand. Soldiers and sailors used to send messages using different flag positions for each letter of the alphabet. The system was called

Flags

Flags aren't limited to making people's arms more noticeable. They have been used for hundreds of years to send messages from one ship to another. Each country used to have its own system, but since

1855 there has been an internationally agreed code so ships from all over the world can understand each other's signals. This code has a different flag for each letter of the alphabet and individual flags for important messages. For instance, this flag ...

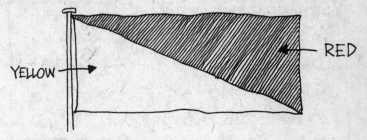

YELLOW

RED

... means either the letter O or "man overboard".

Sound

Horns, drums, whistles, bugles and bells can all send coded messages that travel much further than the human voice. Dogs can learn to understand them too. If you watch a sheepdog trial, you will see shepherds using whistled signals to tell the dogs how to drive the sheep. The shepherd uses a different whistle code for each of his dogs so they can work together without getting in a muddle.

Electricity

The invention of the telegraph in the 1830s introduced a brand-new way to send messages – electricity. The system wasn't very sophisticated so there were only two alternatives – either there was an electric current going down the wire or there wasn't. You couldn't vary the size of the current but you could vary the length of time for which it flowed.

Samuel Morse, the telegraph's inventor, devised a system of dots and dashes to make it work. The telegraph operator pressed a key to send the current down the line – a short press for a dot or one three times as long for a dash.

MORSE CODE

A ∙ —	B — ∙ ∙ ∙	C — ∙ — ∙
D — ∙ ∙	E ∙	F ∙ ∙ — ∙
G — — ∙	H ∙ ∙ ∙ ∙	I ∙ ∙
J ∙ — — —	K — ∙ —	L ∙ — ∙ ∙
M — —	N — ∙	O — — —
P ∙ — — ∙	Q — — ∙ —	R ∙ — ∙
S ∙ ∙ ∙	T —	U ∙ ∙ —
V ∙ ∙ ∙ —	W ∙ — —	X — ∙ ∙ —
Y — ∙ — —	Z — — ∙ ∙	

Did you know?
Morse Code also works well with flashing lights. You can try sending messages to a friend with a torch.

The best known codes
Although fires, flags and whistles are useful at times, the vast majority of codes and ciphers are written down. In fact, you're using one of the best known ciphers at this very moment. If you didn't know it, you wouldn't be able to read this book.

It's the Roman alphabet.

WAIT A MINUTE. THAT'S NOT SECRET!

No, it's not, but the fact that millions of people know it doesn't stop it being a cipher.

Here is an important message from Luke:

КАПТАИН КРИПТИК ИЗ ДАНЖЕРУС

That looks pretty mysterious but it's not. Luke has just written his message in a different alphabet. It's the Cyrillic one and that's not secret either – everyone in Russia knows it. But you probably don't, so you can't understand his message until he shows you the plaintext.

Captain Cryptic is dangerous.

REPORT

- Occupation: Criminal Mastermind.
- Interests: Stealing (particularly art treasures), amassing large fortunes, creating insane plots,
- cackling maniacally and keeping
- tropical fish.

29

It's all Greek to me

Roman Emperor Julius Caesar made good use of a different alphabet while he was trying to keep control of Gaul in around 54 BC. His mate Cicero was surrounded by rebel forces so Caesar and his army set off to rescue him. They would have marched a long way for nothing if Cicero had surrendered before they arrived, so Caesar sent a letter on ahead telling him they were on their way. But Caesar wasn't stupid. He didn't want the rebels to be able to read the letter if they got hold of it, so he used the Greek alphabet instead of the usual Roman one. Luckily for him, none of the rebels could read Greek.

Forgotten secrets

Writing isn't secret. But if everyone forgot what the letters of the alphabet meant, even this book would become completely indecipherable. That may sound far-fetched but it's not. Something very similar happened in the past.

The Great Hieroglyphics Mystery

The ancient Egyptians used a type of writing called hieroglyphics. It was based on small pictures and looked like this.

Sometimes they wrote in columns and sometimes they wrote in rows. The columns were always read from top to bottom but, to make life more confusing, the rows were sometimes read from left to right and sometimes from right to left. You could tell which way to read by seeing which way the animals and birds in that row were facing.

TURN AROUND - YOU'LL GET EVERYONE CONFUSED!

For 3,000 years, the Egyptians used hieroglyphics to write messages on statues, jewellery, tombs and palaces. But gradually they started to use Greek letters instead. The priests were the last to change, but around 400 AD even they stopped using hieroglyphics. No one learnt about them any more, so before long there was no one left who knew how to read them. Hieroglyphics had become a secret code.

Of course, the inscriptions were still there. The tiny pictures looked as if they might be symbols for objects and ideas and, for hundreds of years, everyone believed this was what they were.

The Rosetta Stone

Archaeologists and historians puzzled over hieroglyphics for hundreds of years, trying to crack their code.

In 1799, they had a breakthrough. Some of Napoleon's soldiers discovered a slab of black rock near a place they called Rosetta.

The same message was carved on the Rosetta Stone three times – once in hieroglyphics, once in Greek and once in another type of Egyptian writing called demotic. This was just what the codebreakers needed. Knowing what these hieroglyphics meant would make it easier to unlock their long-forgotten secret.

ROSETTA STONE

ROSETTA JONES

A British scientist called Thomas Young heard about the Stone and got hold of a copy of the inscriptions. He wasn't convinced that the symbols stood for ideas and objects. He thought at least some of them might stand for sounds. So, in 1814, he set out to discover if he was right.

First he found the name of the Pharaoh Ptolemaios in the Greek text. This gave him what codebreakers call a *crib* – a word he could search for in the hieroglyphics because he knew it must be there.

Next he noticed that some of the hieroglyphics were surrounded by an oval (called a *cartouche*). He guessed this might be what he was looking for – the pharaoh's name.

Young tried match to the hieroglyphics inside the oval with the sounds of "Ptolemaios". It worked out like this:

$$\square = P \qquad \triangle = T \qquad \text{[glyph]} = O$$

$$\text{[lion]} = L \qquad \subset = M$$

$$\text{[reeds]} = E \qquad \text{[hook]} = S$$

Young had proved his idea was right. Some hieroglyphics did represent sounds. He continued to work on the Stone for a while but then he stopped for a bit of a rest. Feeling quite pleased with himself, he published the results he'd come up with so far. Although he had made a huge step forward in understanding hieroglyphics, he hadn't completely cracked their code.

Finishing the task Young had started needed someone with passion, determination and skill. That someone was a Frenchman called Jean-Francois Champollion, who had first seen hieroglyphics when he was 10 – just a year or two after the discovery of the Rosetta Stone.

HIEROGLYPHIC INSCRIPTIONS ARE GROOVY. I'M GOING TO WORK OUT HOW TO READ THEM.

To help with his task, Champollion studied lots of languages including Coptic, the closest known language to ancient Egyptian, and he found out everything he could about ancient Egypt. Using that knowledge, he studied the Rosetta Stone himself and agreed with Young's dicoveries. But he didn't want to stop there. He wanted to find out everything about hieroglyphics.

Luckily, in 1822, a friend sent him another inscription with Greek text and hieroglyphics. The timing was perfect – it was just what Champollion needed. The new inscription contained the names Ptolemaios and Cleopatra, and once again they were easy to spot because they were written inside cartouches. Champollion compared the two names and managed to work out what the symbols for Cleopatra meant.

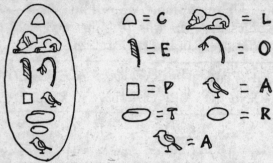

But he still hadn't cracked the code. There was one big snag. Ptolemaios and Cleopatra weren't Egyptian names. Maybe hieroglyphics only stood for sounds when people were writing foreign words.

The only way Champollion could prove this wasn't true was to find an Egyptian name spelt in the same way. But he couldn't find that on the Rosetta Stone or on the inscription his friend had sent to him.

The really big breakthrough happened later the same year. In yet another inscription, he found yet another set of hieroglyphics surrounded by a cartouche.

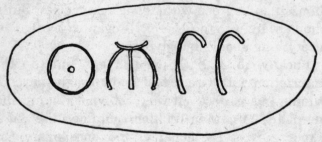

He already knew that the signs at the end meant S but he didn't know the others. Then he had two brainwaves in swift succession.

BRAINWAVE NO: 1

THE FIRST SIGN LOOKS LIKE A SUN AND THE COPTIC WORD FOR SUN IS RA.

WHICH PHARAOH'S NAME BEGINS WITH RA AND ENDS WITH DOUBLE S?

BRAINWAVE NO: 2

RAMESES!

Rameses was one of the most famous of all the pharaohs. Better still, his name was definitely Egyptian. Champollion had proved hieroglyphics stood for sounds in Egyptian words too.

He rushed and told his brother that he had finally cracked the code. Then he fainted – he did that quite often.

As soon as he recovered, Champollion went back to his task until, in 1824, he published a book sharing his discoveries with the world. He had finally achieved his ambition – he had cracked the hieroglyphics code and unlocked the secrets of ancient Egypt.

Hidden Messages

One way to keep a message secret is to hide it so only the person you send it to can find it. In ancient Greece, a leader called Harpagus put a note inside a dead hare carried by a hunter. His enemies saw nothing suspicious and let the hunter go past, so the rather smelly message was delivered safely.

Another ancient Greek called Histaiaeus shaved the head of one of his slaves and wrote a secret message on his scalp. Then he waited for the hair to grow back before sending the slave to his son-in-law with instructions to shave his head.

SLAP THIS ON. IT'S AN URGENT MESSAGE!

It's a good idea to hide your secret message, even if it's written in code. Even the cleverest codebreakers can't crack it if they haven't seen it.

Twentieth-century spies hid messages in brushes with hollow handles, fake batteries that were hollow inside and holes carved in gateposts. (Of course, the gateposts were too heavy to carry around – spies used them as postboxes where they could leave a message for someone else to collect.)

Modern spies often photograph secret information onto tiny pieces of film so they can fit into even smaller places. Sometimes these are so small that they could replace one of the full stops in this book. Using one of these microdots, you could send Luke an ordinary letter with a secret film hiding in the punctuation.

The note in a nickel

Hiding messages in ordinary-looking objects is fine until you lose them (which is pretty hard to do with a gatepost). In 1953 a boy called Jimmy Bozart was selling newspapers in New York when he dropped a nickel on the floor. To his  amazement, the coin split in half. Inside it, he found a piece of film about one centimetre square with a picture of rows of numbers. It was a secret message written in code.

Jimmy gave the film to the police, who handed it on to the FBI. But none of their experts could crack the code, so, for four years, no one knew what the message said.

Then the codebreakers had some good luck. A Russian secret agent changed sides and told the Americans how the code worked. At long last, they could read the note in the nickel. But sadly it didn't contain any earth-shattering information. It was just a welcome letter to a newly arrived spy!

Invisible ink

If you don't want to hide your message inside something, you could try writing it in invisible ink. Lemon juice and vinegar have both been used since Roman times. Anything written using them looks invisible when dry but turns brown when the paper is warmed.

Of course, spies don't always have a lemon or bottle of vinegar handy. But there's another natural invisible ink they can always get hold of even if they are caught, and especially if they are caught short. It's urine!

Messages within messages

Imagine you are working undercover to defeat Captain Cryptic's plans for his next big robbery. You need to report back to Luke but you know the captain and his assistant, Tibbs, are checking all the letters you send. Writing a message that is obviously in code will immediately arouse their suspicions. Even invisible ink won't work because they are testing all your letters for it.

The answer is to hide your secret message within a perfectly innocent-looking one. That may sound difficult but there are several different ways to do it.

Marking letters

For this method, you need an ordinary newspaper and a pin. You spell out your message by pricking a tiny hole under the appropriate letters in the paper.

Politicians and secret agents are annoyed at the publication of an amazing new book called *Cracking Codes*. "Secret codes should remain secret forever," whispered one spy. "ODVLXPZEJINYQ," said an expert in ciphers.

(As we're not allowed to make holes in this book, we have put dots under the letters instead.)

Now send the paper to Luke. The captain and Tibbs won't spot your message when they look at it in the normal way. But Luke can work it out by holding the paper up to the light so he can see the holes.

If you don't have a convenient newspaper, you could write Luke a completely innocent note and use the pinprick technique to mark letters in that instead. If you prefer, you could mark the letters by writing them very slightly lower than the others or by printing them in a different typeface. But it's difficult to do that without making it look really obvious.

Adding extra letters

Adding extra letters, called "nulls", to a message makes it much harder to read. For instance, this message makes no sense unless you know that you should only read alternate letters.

```
TAHPICSRWEONRAKTSERIEJAPLRLTYAWOEKLNLY
```

Unfortunately, this kind of message looks very suspicious so it will immediately attract the captain's attention. You need to choose the extra letters so they spell out an innocent-looking message that contains your secret one in a prearranged pattern. For instance, in this note, the important letters are the first one in each sentence.

How are you? Everything is going well here. Lunch was lovely today. Perhaps tomorrow's will be too. Most meals here are good. Eventually I'll put on so much weight that I'll have to go on a diet.

If you want to make your message even harder to spot, you can use the second or third letters of the words or sentences instead of the first ones.

This way of hiding a message is particularly useful in wartime when the authorities check letters for sensitive information. It's been used by spies to send reports on ship movements and by soldiers who wanted to tell their families where they are. But it can also help magicians perform mind-reading acts.

The Mysterious Mind-Reading Trick

How the trick looks to the audience

You ask a volunteer from the audience to lend you a coin. You don't touch it at all and neither does your assistant, but other members of the audience are allowed to check there is nothing extraordinary about it.

Five other volunteers come forward to form a panel sitting on chairs facing the audience. You leave the room while the volunteer chooses one member of the panel and gives him or her the coin to sit on or put in a pocket.

Once everyone is settled again, your assistant calls you back into the room. You make a great show of going to each panel member in turn, holding your hands over their heads so you can read their minds to detect the coin. Finally you select the correct panel member.

What really happens

Before you begin your trick, you agree a keyword
with your assistant. Any word will do as long as
it has no duplicated letters. In this case, the
keyword is TIGER, which has five letters, so you
pick five panel members. If the keyword had
been HANDLE, you would have needed six
volunteers.

In your mind, you give one letter to each of the
panel members like this:

When your assistant calls you in, the first
word that he or she says begins with the letter
belonging to the chosen person. For instance:

"**T**ime to come back in," for person one.

"**I** think we're ready," for person two.

"**G**reat news – we're ready for you now," for
person three.

"**E**veryone's ready," for person four.

"**R**eady," for person five.

You know who it is before you come into the room.
All the hand-waving and other mumbo-jumbo is
an act to make the audience believe it's magic.

The Big Snag

Using extra words to disguise your message works best for fairly short messages hidden in fairly long letters. Short letters designed to hold long messages tend to sound very contrived, like this one:

> The inspector brought bananas safely home after sampling pears, lemons and nine strawberries.

In wartime, censors check all the mail to make sure no one is passing information to the enemy. When they see a letter that sounds strange or awkward, the codebreakers write it in different ways to see if they can spot a hidden message. They could easily find out the secret of that strange sentence by writing all the words underneath each other:

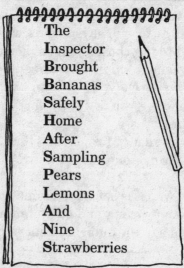

The
Inspector
Brought
Bananas
Safely
Home
After
Sampling
Pears
Lemons
And
Nine
Strawberries

All the hidden messages in this chapter have been in clear so anyone who finds them can read them easily. That's fine if you are just sending messages for fun but it's not so good for real secrets. For those, you need to follow the example of the spy with the hollow coin and use some kind of cipher or secret code. So let's take a look at how they work.

Simple Ciphers

There are two completely different kinds of cipher.

Both kinds have been used since ancient times, but for the moment let's concentrate on substitution ciphers. (We'll get to the others in the chapter after next.)

In theory, you can use any symbols you like so there is nothing actually wrong with a cipher like this:

```
Plain   a b c d e f g h i j k l m n o p q r s t u v w x y z
Cipher  = % $ # @ ! ^ & * > ? < \ © ± » ® ÷ µ ] § [ / Ø æ ¿
```

The trouble is it's hard to remember which of those symbols belongs with each letter. That means you would have to keep a written copy to help you encipher your messages and Luke would need a copy too so he could decipher them. If either copy fell into Captain Cryptic's hands, he would be able to decipher them too, so none of your secrets would be secret any longer.

It's much better to use a cipher that is easy to remember so you don't need to keep a written record.

The pigpen cipher

One cipher which uses strange-looking symbols has been around for hundreds of years. No one knows for sure when the pigpen cipher was first invented but it was used by a secret society called the Freemasons in the eighteenth century, by Confederate soldiers in the American Civil War and, more recently, by shopkeepers to mark their stock with information they didn't want their customers to read.

To work out the cipher alphabet, you write the letters of the ordinary alphabet in a series of grids like this:

A	B	C
D	E	F
G	H	I

N	O	P
Q	R	S
T	U	V

J
K · L
M

W
X · · Y
Z

The symbol for each letter shows its position in the grids. So ☐ means E, ∧ means M and ◆ means X. The complete cipher alphabet looks like this.

A B C D E F G H I J K L M

N O P Q R S T U V W X Y Z

It's a good thing you've learnt that because Luke has just sent you this message.

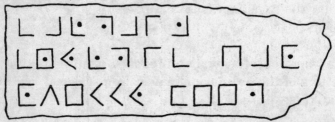

Luke's pigpen message says: "Captain Cryptic has smelly feet."

You can make the pigpen cipher harder to crack by writing the letters in a different order but it is still too well known for really important secret messages.

50

The Polybius Checkerboard

Another cipher based on a diagram was invented thousands of years ago by an ancient Greek called Polybius.

He wrote the alphabet in a grid five rows high and five columns wide. As the Greek alphabet has only 24 letters, it fitted easily with one square left over. However our alphabet has 26 letters so one square has to hold two letters. Usually these are I and J, so the completed grid looks like this.

	1	2	3	4	5
1	A	B	C	D	E
2	F	G	H	IJ	K
3	L	M	N	O	P
4	Q	R	S	T	U
5	V	W	X	Y	Z

If you were sending your message in Russian, you would need a 6x6 checkerboard because there are 33 letters in the Cyrillic alphabet.

Each letter is represented by the pair of numbers which show its position on the checkerboard, with the row number first. So B is 12, P is 35 and X is 53.

Knock, knock – who's there?

The Polybius square is the basis of the knock cipher – a system used for centuries in dungeons and jails. The prisoners tapped out their messages on their cell walls, leaving a slight pause between the two numbers which made up a letter and a longer pause between the letters themselves. It worked something like this. (Each letter starts on a new line.)

Tap tap   tap tap tap
Tap   tap tap tap tap tap
Tap tap tap   tap
Tap tap tap   tap
Tap tap tap   tap tap tap tap

The knock cipher message says: "Hello."

Caesar's ciphers

Julius Caesar didn't just use the Greek alphabet to help him send secret messages – as we saw on page 30. His best-known technique involved replacing each letter in his message by the one three places further on in the alphabet.

Plain a b c d e f g h i j k l m n o p q r s t u v w x y z
Cipher D E F G H I J K L M N O P Q R S T U V W X Y Z A B C

Using this cipher his name would look like this:

MXOLXV FDHVDU

This kind of cipher is called a Caesar shift for obvious reasons. You don't have to restrict yourself to moving the letters three places along. You can move them any number you like.

The Good News
As long as Luke knows the number too, he can write out the cipher whenever he needs to decipher one of your messages. Provided you both destroy the cipher when you have finished with it, there is nothing for the captain or anyone else to find.

The Bad News
There are only 26 possible Caesar shifts, including one that's completely useless as it's identical to the original alphabet. Once the captain realizes you are using this method, he only has to try each possible shift in turn until he finds the one that works.

Keywords
Another way to make an easy-to-remember cipher alphabet is to use a key. First of all, you need to agree on a word, a phrase or some other sequence of letters which neither of you is likely to forget. Then you write it at the beginning of your cipher

alphabet, leaving out any repeats of a letter you have already used.

If you have agreed with Luke that your key is "cat food", you miss out the second O and write this:

```
Plain   a b c d e f g h i j k l m n o p q r s t u v w x y z
Cipher  C A T F O D
```

Then you fill in the rest of the alphabet in order, starting from the last letter of the keyword and missing out any letters you have already used.

```
Plain   a b c d e f g h i j k l m n o p q r s t u v w x y z
Cipher  C A T F O D E G H I J K L M N P Q R S U V W X Y Z B
```

Provided you remember the key, you can recreate the cipher alphabet any time you like. That means you don't need to keep it written down, so there is nothing for Captain Cryptic to find. Better still, it's almost impossible to break the code by trying all the possible cipher alphabets in turn because there are more than 400,000,000,000,000,000,000,000,000 to choose from.

You're dying to know why, aren't you?

When you choose the first letter in your cipher alphabet, you can choose any of the 26 letters available. When you choose the second, one's already been used so you have a choice of the remaining 25. For the third, you have a choice of 24 and so on.

So the number of possible cipher alphabets is:

26 x 25 x 24 x 23 x ... and so on, right down to x 3 x 2 x 1 which makes:
403,291,461,126,605,635,584,000,000

The first crack

For over 2,000 years, the codemakers had everything their own way.

Although the Greeks and Romans used ciphers, they didn't have any method for deciphering ones they didn't know. They had to rely on lucky guesses to help them work out the meaning or persuade the messengers to let them in on the secret.

I WON'T STOP UNTIL YOU TELL ME...

But then something happened to knock the codemakers' confidence. During the eighth and nineth centuries AD, the Arabs were busy studying written language. As part of that process, they counted the frequency of letters (how often each letter appears in any piece of writing) and discovered that some were used more often than others. More importantly, the most frequently used letters were the same in any large piece of writing in the same language.

No one knows for sure exactly when they realized this discovery could help to crack codes. But when they did, they created the art of cryptanalysis (the posh name for codebreaking). They also created one of its most powerful tools – frequency analysis.

To use it, you count how many times each letter appears in the secret message you want to crack. Then you compare your answer with the normal frequency of the letters in the same language.

If you don't know which language the message is in, the frequency analysis can sometimes help you decide.

Unfortunately, this method isn't foolproof. There is always the chance that the original message had an unusual letter distribution.

Did you know?

E is the most frequent letter in both English and French. But in 1969, Georges Perec managed to write an entire novel in French containing no E's at all. It was called La Disparition *which means* The Disappearance. *The book was translated into English too, but the English version is called* A Void *to avoid using Es.*

EEEEE...THIS IS SPOOKY!

Despite that problem, frequency analysis is a valuable tool for codebreakers. It can help them find a chink in a cipher which they can use to crack it.

Unlocking a secret

Luke has managed to intercept this message from Tibbs to Captain Cryptic.

```
SUTJ  BTGLTYE  BJQGLYB  KUNUELUUE  IFPUK
FV  ZUOUCK  TJU  IUYEW  KUEL  LF  VJTEBU  FE
OUSEUKSTQ  Y  BTE  KLUTC  LXUD  OYLX  LXU
XUCG  FV  LXJUU  DUE  TES  T  WULTOTQ  BTJ
IUKL  OYKXUK  LYIIK
```

Tibbs isn't very good at foreign languages so he is sure to have written the original message in English. Luckily he is not very good at codes either so he will only have used a simple cipher. Even so, the coded message looks completely meaningless. Let's try to help Luke decipher it.

I've started by counting the frequency of all the letters. U crops up much more often than any other letter. So we're going to guess that it stands for e, because e is the most frequently used letter in the English language.

Don't worry that this is just a guess. If it turns out to be wrong, we can always go back and start again. Codebreaking often involves lots of guesses and false starts.

"I" and "a" are the only one-letter words in English. Let's see if Tibbs has used them. If he has, we'll know which cipher letters stand for them.

We're in luck. Y and T are both in the message on their own. That means one of them stands for i and the other one stands for a, but we don't know which is which. We need to find something else in the message that can help us work it out.

The first word of the message is SUTJ and, if our decision about U is right, the UT must mean either ei or ea.

So we need to think of a four-letter word that has ei or ea in the middle that might be at the beginning of a message...

Great. If the first word is "dear", T must mean a, so Y means i. Also S means d, and J means r.

Now we need to think what might follow "dear". So let's take a look at the first three words of Tibbs' message to see what we already know.

```
Plain  dear   a ai  r i
Cipher SUTJ  BTGLTYE  BJQGLYB
```

The a's, i's and r are just where we would expect them to be if the second and third words were "Captain Cryptic". There's another clue too – both words start with the same letter and the second word ends in that same letter.

"Captain Cryptic" fits and gives us the meaning of more of the letters!

It looks as if we're really getting somewhere. Now, if Tibbs has started the letter with "Dear Captain Cryptic", maybe he's ended it with his own name. Let's look at the last word in the message and see what we already know about it.

```
Plain   ti
Cipher  LYIIK
```

It begins with ti and there's a double letter in the right place too. So it looks as if the last word really is "Tibbs".

Now we know what four of the words mean, we also know the meaning of all the letters in those words. Let's write them in and see how much of the rest of the message we can understand.

```
dear   captain  cryptic  se    enteen  b   es
SUTJ   BTGLTYE  BJQGLYB  KUNUELUUE    IFPUK

    e e s  are  bein   sent  t     rance  n
FV  ZUOUCK  TJU  IUYEW  KUEL  LF  VJTEBU  FE

    ednesday  I  can  stea   t e   it  t e
OUSEUKSTQ  Y  BTE  KLUTC  LXUD  OYLX  LXU

     e p    t ree  en   and  a   eta  ay car
XUCG  FV  LXJUU  DUE  TES  T  WULTOTQ  BTJ

best   is  es  tibbs
IUKL  OYKXUK  LYIIK
```

60

Isn't it amazing how much we already know?

We could go on guessing other words in the message, but first let's take a look at how much of the cipher alphabet we've discovered and see if we can guess the key.

Plain   a b c d e f g h i j k l m n o p q r s t u v w x y z
Cipher   T I B S U   Y   E   G   J K L   Q

This time we're really in luck. That idiot Tibbs has used his own name as the key.

Tibbs has remembered to use the double letter only once, so from U onwards, the cipher alphabet is in alphabetical order. We can easily fill in the gaps and decipher the rest of the message.

If you don't want to work it out for yourself, the answer's over the page...

Cracking that cipher was stunningly simple. But Tibbs is one of the worst secret agents in the world. He made several coding mistakes that made our job easier:

He left the gaps between the words.
This helped us to spot the one-letter words so we could immediately identify the cipher letters for *a* and *i*. It also helped us pick out individual words like *Captain*, *Cryptic* and *Tibbs*.

To stop codebreakers doing this, clever codemakers take out the normal gaps so the words run together. Then they break the ciphertext into groups of five or six characters.

This even makes an uncoded message look confusing.

```
THISM ESSAG EISNO TINCO DEBUT ITISH
ARDTO READ
```

He used predictable words in predictable places.
By being so polite, Tibbs made it easy for us to guess the beginning and end of the message. Once we had done that, we were able to work out the meanings of

62

the cipher letters in those words and use them to crack the code.

To stop this happening, cunning codemakers avoid using predictable phrases as much as they can. But even experienced ones sometimes fall into this trap.

Did you know?

During the First World War, a German officer called Lieutenant Jaegar kept writing to his troops encouraging them to improve their use of codes. But his messages did less good than he had hoped. By putting his name at the end of each one, he accidentally gave the other side a crib which helped them crack the codes he was trying to protect.

THANK YOU, LIEUTENANT JAEGAR!

PHOOEY!

He chose a short key.

By using a short key, Tibbs created a cipher alphabet where the majority of the letters were in alphabetical order. That made it easy to spot the codeword and to guess the cipher letters we hadn't already found. Cunning codemakers use longer keys because they are usually harder to crack.

He chose an obvious key.

We managed to work out the whole key from the words we knew. But even if we had only worked out two or three of the letters, we could have guessed the key easily because it was an obvious word. You would have found it much harder if Tibbs had used a random sequence of letters as his key. The trouble is, it's difficult to remember something like SQHYTPKBX.

Beating the frequency count

It wasn't Tibbs' fault that we could use a frequency count to crack his code. That's a basic snag with all ciphers which use just one symbol to replace each letter of the alphabet.

Cunning codemakers always look for ways to beat the frequency count problem. One way they can do that is by using a code instead of a cipher.

codenames and code talkers

Proper codes replace whole words with other words, numbers or groups of letters that don't spell words. As a result, the letter frequency in the coded message is completely different from that of the plaintext. So there is no way a frequency count can help you to crack a code, and if it uses numbers, there aren't even any letters to count.

There's one big snag. If you want your code to handle every possible situation, you need a codebook that lists alternatives for every single word in the dictionary plus the name of every place in the world plus every possible name for a person, a dog, a cat, a horse, a hamster or anything else. That's an awful lot of words, so your codebook would be enormously big, ridiculously heavy and impossible to hide.

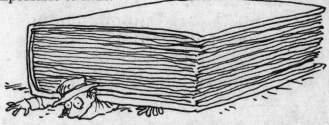

To avoid this problem, codemakers compromise. They create alternatives for the most likely or most important words and use some kind of cipher for the others. Sometimes, they even write the less important words in clear, like Swingle did in his recipe on page 24.

Secret systems that combined a code with a cipher were particularly popular from around 1400 onwards. Kings, queens and diplomats loved them. They also liked long words so they called their systems nomenclators.

The queen who trusted codes too much

The fact that you can't use frequency analysis to crack codes doesn't mean they are completely safe. Cribs, lucky guesses and stolen codebooks can all help unlock their secrets.

Many people through the ages have believed their system was uncrackable. Unfortunately some of them have found out the hard way that they were wrong. One of these was Mary Queen of Scots.

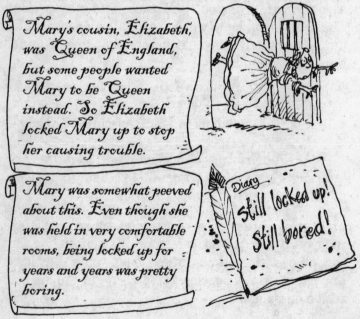

Mary's cousin, Elizabeth, was Queen of England, but some people wanted Mary to be Queen instead. So Elizabeth locked Mary up to stop her causing trouble.

Mary was somewhat peeved about this. Even though she was held in very comfortable rooms, being locked up for years and years was pretty boring.

Diary
Still locked up!
Still bored!

She brightened up when a man called Gilbert Gifford worked out a way to smuggle letters in and out of her prison in barrels of beer.

SHE'S REALLY GETTING THROUGH THIS BEER!

Mary was cunning. She guessed the letters might fall into the wrong hands.

I'LL WRITE IN THIS TERRIFIC CODE, IT'S UNCRACKABLE.

Oops! Mary was horribly wrong. Her code looked complicated but it definitely wasn't uncrackable.

It was a nomenclator made up from:

- a cipher with one symbol for each letter of the alphabet
- a few meaningless extra symbols (nulls) to confuse the codebreakers
- a code with symbols to stand for certain words.

Unfortunately Mary's codemakers weren't very cunning so they made a big mistake. They only used symbols to replace really common words like *the*, *and* and *when*. Important words like *kill*, *murder* and *escape* all had to be spelled out in cipher and so did all the names. That was a daft idea. Once the codebreakers cracked the cipher, they could read all the important words and easily guess the others.

This was great for Elizabeth but fatal for Mary.

Tudor Times

MARY LOSES HER HEAD OVER CODE

Mary, Queen of Scots, finally lost her head yesterday. The scheming royal had plotted to kill our beloved Queen Elizabeth. But she had underestimated the palace codebreakers. They cunningly cracked correspondence handed over by double agent Gilbert Gifford, and revealed her wicked plans for all to see. The *Times* says, "Serves you right, Mary." God save the Queen!

The uncracked royal code

Mary wasn't the only royal prisoner to use a code and she wasn't the only one to lose her head either. In 1648, Charles I was locked up in Carisbrooke Castle on the Isle of Wight. He was fed up because he'd just lost the Civil War and he wanted to escape.

Like Mary, he plotted and schemed with friends outside. Like Mary, he used a code to hide his plans from prying eyes. But his code was better than hers. It used numbers to stand for words and it's never been cracked. Even modern codebreakers can't decode the letter he sent just before his planned breakout.

(If you think you could do better, you can see the letter in the castle's museum.)

The uncracked code kept his letter secret but the escape plan still failed. It depended on two sentries he had bribed to help him, but they changed their minds and warned the other guards. So, like Mary, he stayed locked up and, like Mary, he eventually had his head chopped off. Which just goes to show that even a really strong code doesn't always solve all your problems.

Code names

As Mary Queen of Scots discovered too late, it's the important words in your message that you need to replace with code. Some of the most important ones are the names of people and places. Replacing those with codenames can make it very hard for outsiders to understand your message.

> Tyrannosaurus to attack pterodactyl's nest at dawn.

That message from Luke sounds like something out of *Jurassic Park*, unless you know that *Tyrannosaurus* is the codename for the Criminal Mastermind Investigation Squad and *pterodactyl's nest* is the codename for Tibbs' hideout.

> Bother. Now everyone knows.

It isn't just people and places that have codenames. Sometimes they are given to events as well. In the Second World War, the allied invasion of France was called *Overlord*, the invasion of North Africa was called *Torch* and the development of the atomic bomb was called the *Manhattan Project*.

The codename advantage

Codenames only work if the opposition doesn't know what they mean. But cunning codebreakers sometimes use tricks to help them find out.

In 1942, the Americans had a problem.

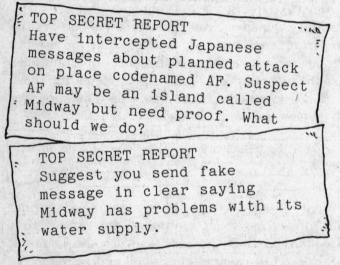

TOP SECRET REPORT
Have intercepted Japanese messages about planned attack on place codenamed AF. Suspect AF may be an island called Midway but need proof. What should we do?

TOP SECRET REPORT
Suggest you send fake message in clear saying Midway has problems with its water supply.

The plan worked. The Japanese picked up the fake message and passed on the information using the codename AF for Midway. Now the Americans knew exactly where the attack would happen and that advance warning helped them win the Battle of Midway.

Telegraph troubles

Before the telegraph arrived in the 1830s, it was fairly easy to send a private message. You wrote a letter, sealed it in an envelope and posted it. If you were just an ordinary person, the letter was very unlikely to be intercepted so you could be confident that no one would read it except the person you sent it to.

The telegraph changed that situation dramatically. You could now send messages quickly to people hundreds of miles away but you couldn't do it privately. That's because the telegraph system worked like this:

YOU WROTE DOWN YOUR MESSAGE...

YOU GAVE IT TO A TELEGRAPH OPERATOR...

THE OPERATOR READ THE MESSAGE AND SENT IT IN MORSE CODE.

TAP! TAP! TAP!

THE OPERATOR AT THE OTHER END RECEIVED THE MORSE CODE AND WROTE DOWN YOUR MESSAGE.

TAP! TAP!

THE TELEGRAM BOY DELIVERED YOUR MESSAGE.

DID YOU READ THIS?

NO!

So your message was always read by at least two telegraph operators. There was no way you could keep its contents secret.

This caused an explosion of interest in codes and ciphers. Until then, they had mainly been used by spies, diplomats and soldiers. Now lovers, businessmen and other ordinary people wanted to use them too.

Money matters

Secrecy wasn't the only reason for the new interest in codes. The other reason was money. Sending telegrams was expensive and the price depended on the number of words in your message. So replacing a whole phrase with a single codeword kept the cost down.

At first, people and companies made up their own codes to help them do this. But it wasn't long before publishers got in on the act and started producing codebooks that everyone could use. These contained one-word alternatives for a dazzling selection of phrases. For instance, *The Unicode Universal Telegraph Code Book*, published in 1897, included:

Ancilla
(CONFINED TODAY TWINS BOTH GIRLS ALL WELL)

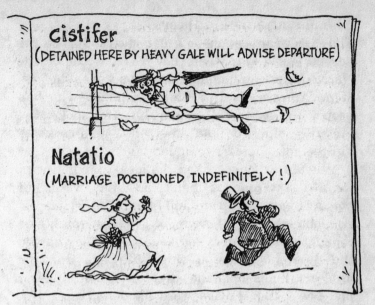

Cistifer
(DETAINED HERE BY HEAVY GALE WILL ADVISE DEPARTURE)

Natatio
(MARRIAGE POSTPONED INDEFINITELY!)

As usual, the code books were very big but, for once, size didn't matter. These books weren't secret so there was no need to hide them.

Language as code

One way to avoid the need for an enormous codebook is to base your code on another language. This method is particularly useful in battlefields. If you are sitting in the mud with bullets whistling past your ears, it's difficult to turn your call for help into a coded message without making mistakes. It's quicker and easier to translate it into another language you know well.

But there's no point in using French or German. Those languages are much too well known. You need to choose one only your side are likely to understand.

The Navaho code talkers

The Americans made a great choice during the Second World War when they based a code on the Native American language Navaho. It was the idea of an American called Philip Johnston who had grown up among the Navaho. He spoke the language fluently and knew it was incredibly difficult for outsiders to understand.

Although it looked liked the ideal starting point for a secret code, it didn't have any words for *machine gun*, *battleship* and other military jargon. So Johnson and a group of Navaho volunteers thought up codewords to use instead. They named the different kinds of ship after fish and the different kinds of plane after birds. So a fighter plane was the Navaho word for a *hummingbird*, while a dive bomber was a *chicken hawk*, a battleship was a *whale* and a destroyer was a *shark*.

Countries had codenames too – Britain was *between waters*, America was *our mother* and Italy, for less obvious reasons, was *stutter*. There were even codewords for punctuation marks – a comma was a *tail drop*.

The code talkers learned the code by heart so there was nothing written down to be captured by the enemy. When they sent a message, they encoded it in their heads and spoke the coded message on the radio. Then the code talker listening at the other end of the line decoded it in the same way. The whole process was much quicker than traditional pencil-and-paper methods. It was also more reliable.

Did you know?
During the fierce battle for Iwo Jima in 1945, the code talkers sent and received over 800 messages without making a single mistake – a huge achievement in such a dangerous situation.

Sometimes the messages contained names and other words with no Navaho code equivalent, so the code talkers needed a way to spell them out. To help them do this, they had a different codeword for each letter in the alphabet. To make that part of the code hard to crack, most letters were represented by a choice of two or three different words so just memorizing the alphabet involved remembering more than 60 words.

But the code talkers did occasionally run into problems. American soldiers who hadn't met Navahos before sometimes thought they were Japanese.

The Navaho code was never broken. It was so important that it remained top secret for many years after the war in case it was ever needed again.

Book codes

Another way to avoid huge codebooks is to base your code on an ordinary book. This is particularly useful if you're a secret agent because you can carry that around without raising anyone's suspicions.

Make sure you and the person you are sending to both use the same edition of the book. A different edition may have the words in different places.

To use the book code to replace a word in your message:

1. Find that word in your book.

2. Write down the page number.

3. Put a full stop.

4. Write down the number of the line it is in, counting the top line as 1.

5. Put another full stop.

6. Write down the number of the word, counting from the left.

So the third word on the fifteenth line of page 340 of your book will have the code 340.15.3.

Book code blues

Book codes sound so easy that you may be wondering why anyone uses anything else. If you want to find out, try using this book to encode "Captain Cryptic wants Tibbs to send him a message in cipher."

IT TAKES AGES TO FIND THE RIGHT WORDS!

The Secret Agent's Handbook

Practice Test – Intermediate Level
You need to use a book code and have three possible books you could use. Which of these would be your best choice?

a) *A Tale of Peter Rabbit* by Beatrix Potter
b) *The Lord of the Rings* by J.R.R. Tolkien
c) *The Concise Oxford Dictionary*

Answers:
a) Much too short, so it's unlikely to contain many of the words you need.
b) A huge selection of words but it's very difficult to find the one you want.
c) A good choice with a wide range of words in alphabetical order.

A dictionary is great choice for a book code. You only use the words that are defined so you don't have to worry about counting along the lines. You just say which column the word is in.

So, if your word is the third one in the second column on page 15, your code would be 15.2.3.

However, even the largest dictionary in the world won't contain every word and name you need. Sometimes you can think of a way round it. For instance, you could split *Stephen* into *step* and *hen*, or you could give people codenames, like *elephant* or *mouse*, that are in the dictionary.

But if neither of those options works, you'll need to spell the names using some kind of cipher. One possible way is to base that on the book too, using just the first letters of words. A book cipher like this is part of a mysterious tale of hidden treasure...

The Mystery of the Hidden Gold
The tale starts in 1817 when an adventurer called Thomas J Beale set off with a group of friends to explore the American West. One night they were camped in a ravine, when suddenly...

For months, the friends worked the goldmine they had stumbled across. Eventually they had a fortune in gold, silver and jewels.

So, in 1820, Beale buried the treasure near Lynchburg, Virginia.

Then he went back to help the others dig up more gold. By 1822, the men had more treasure to hide. But by now they had thought of something important.

So this time, after Beale had buried their latest riches with the rest of their hoard, he wrote instructions on how to find it. But, to keep them from prying eyes, he wrote the instructions in cipher and locked them in a metal box which he asked a local innkeeper, Robert Morriss, to look after for him.

After he set off for the mine again, Beale wrote to Morriss telling him to open the box in ten years' time if no one had collected it. He also promised that someone would send him the key to the cipher.

Beale rode off and...

No one knows what happened to him. Nothing was ever heard of him again. No one collected the box and no one sent Morriss the key.

Morriss waited ...

       ... and waited ...

              ... and waited for 23 years.

Then he opened the box and found three messages in cipher. A letter in clear explained that one cipher described *where* the treasure was, one *what* it was and one *whose* it was.

The great treasure hunt

Morriss couldn't crack the ciphers so he gave them to a friend who knew about codes. That friend managed to crack the one that described the treasure. It was written in a book cipher based on the Declaration of Independence. The words in the Declaration were numbered in order and each number in the message stood for the first letter of that word.

The Declaration begins:

When   in   the   course   of   human   events...
  1   2   3   4   5   6   7

So 1,6,2,4,6 means *which*.

But the Declaration of Independence didn't help decipher the other two messages. So Morriss still couldn't find Beale's treasure.

After Morriss died, his friend decided to publish the ciphers to see if anyone else could succeed where he had failed. His pamphlet came out in 1885 and it has intrigued codebreakers and treasure hunters ever since.

They have tried loads of different ways to crack the codes and dug lots of holes in Virginia. Some people even claim to have found a solution. But none of them have become multi-millionaires as a result, which suggests no one has yet found the treasure.

The two uncracked ciphers might be based on other pieces of well-known writing, but no one has yet found anything that works. Alternatively Beale may have written something himself on which to base them. That writing could be the key that was never delivered.

But the other possibility is that the whole story is a hoax set up to fool people and make money by selling the original pamphlet. Maybe there isn't any treasure. Maybe Thomas Beale, the box and Robert Morriss never existed. What do you think?

Juggling Letters

Not all ciphers replace letters with other symbols. Transposition ciphers leave the letters exactly the same. They just put them in a different order.

Tibbs thinks this is an excellent idea, so he's mixed up the letters of his latest message to Captain Cryptic to form an anagram.

HEDELMPOSNER

Unfortunately Tibbs didn't tell his boss how to unscramble his message. But it isn't very long so the captain is sure he'll be able to guess what it means. He finds plenty of hidden words...

Then he finds the solution.

"Aha!" laughs the captain in suitably evil tones. "Mrs Deel must be about to make a deal. Maybe she's ready to pay the ransom for her stolen painting." Rubbing his hands at the thought of all that cash, he reaches for the phone.

Meanwhile Tibbs has his own problems to worry about.

Tibbs' mistake was not agreeing with the captain in advance how he would jumble up the letters in the message. If he had, the captain would have worked out the right message straight away.

Letter juggling for beginners

The easiest way to juggle a message is to write it back to front. This is even more effective if you take out the spaces between the words and break the resulting string of letters into groups of five.

```
ELBUO RTYNA TUOHT IWTIK CARCL LIWRE
KAERB EDOCA TUBYL ISAET IGNID AEREL
POEPS POTSS IHT
```

Zig-zags and rail fences

Suppose you want to tell Luke, "Diamonds being moved tonight." It's important the captain doesn't find out, so you need to jumble the letters to hide your message from Tibbs' prying eyes.

One way to do this is to write the message in a zig-zag like this.

```
D A O D B I G O E T N G T
 I M N S E N M V D O I H
```

To create your coded message (or ciphertext), just write down the top line first followed by the bottom line. You can group the letters into fives if you like – it makes them easier to copy and easier to send by radio.

```
DAODB IGOET NGTIM NSENM VDOIH
```

To decipher your message, Luke just has to repeat the process backwards. Your ciphertext has an odd number of letters, so he knows the top line is one letter longer than the bottom line. (If it had an even number, both lines would be the same length.) Using that knowledge, he can divide the letters into two groups, write them down to recreate your original diagram and read along the zig-zag to discover your message.

He has used exactly the same method to send you his reply.

```
CLPLC  IYUEC  PANRP  IALOI  EFOSE
ATICY TC
```

This way of juggling or transposing letters is called a rail fence cipher because some people think the zig-zag arrangement looks vaguely like a fence. If you want to make it harder, you can have three or more levels to the zig-zag instead of only two. You can also write one or more of the lines backwards. But don't forget to make sure Luke knows what you've done so he can decipher it easily.

Columns and rows

Rail fence ciphers aren't the only way to jumble a message by writing it in a particular way. To keep the captain guessing you are going to use a different method – one that uses rows and columns.

Your message is:

```
Have  spotted  Tibbs  creeping  around
the Tower of London.
```

You've already agreed with Luke that you will base your cipher on the number 5, so you need to make a grid with five columns and write your message along the rows. Don't worry if the last row isn't full.

```
H A V E S
P O T T E
D T I B B
S C R E E
P I N G A
R O U N D
T H E T O
W E R O F
L O N D O
N
```

To create the ciphertext, write down the letters in each column one after the other like this.

HPDSPRTWLNAOTCIOHEOVTIRNUERNETBEGNTOD
SEBEADOFO

As usual, you can divide that into five-letter groups to make it easier to copy and send.

HPDSP RTWLN AOTCI OHEOV TIRNU ERNET
BEGNT ODSEB EADOF O

Luke can decode the message because he knows you have used five columns. First of all, he counts how many letters there are in the message (46). Then he divides that number by five to see how many rows you had. (46÷5=9 with one letter left over, so there are nine full rows and one row that has only one letter.) Once he knows that, he can draw a grid the right size, copy in your ciphertext by writing down the columns and discover your message by reading along the rows.

You can use exactly the same technique to decipher his reply.

```
WPDPH  TLOLR  EEOIE  EAAST  OWLTS  CCINT
HWELT  UTANS  EENLS  ESTPP  TACJS
```

Answer: *Well spotted. I suspect the captain plans to steal the crown jewels.*

The codebreakers are right again. Although Luke's message looks impenetrable, the captain can work out what it says by trial and error. Luke started by writing the first column so the first letter of the ciphertext is also the first letter of your message.

The captain only has to experiment with different-sized grids to see which ones give him real words when he reads across the rows. That sounds as if it would take ages, but it won't. He'll be able to eliminate most of the grids by just looking at the first two letters on the first line. You can try it yourself and see.

Key complications

You can make this kind of transposition code much harder to crack if you don't write the columns in order from left to right. But it's important that Luke knows the order you have used. As it's difficult to remember a string of numbers, it's easier to use a keyword or phrase you both know.

To get the order for writing the columns from your key, you number the letters in the word or phrase in alphabetical order. If the same letter crops up more than once, number the one on the left first, then the next on the right and so on. So if your key is "*cat food*", the numbers look like this.

```
C  A  T  F  O  O  D
2  1  7  4  5  6  3
```

Your key has seven letters so your next step is to write the plaintext of your message in seven columns with the numbers from the key along the top. So, the message "Tibbs is hiding in the dungeons. Should I fetch police" would look like this.

```
2  1  7  4  5  6  3
T  I  B  B  S  I  S
H  I  D  I  N  G  I
N  T  H  E  D  U  N
G  E  O  N  S  S  H
O  U  L  D  I  F  E
T  C  H  P  O  L  I
C  E
```

Your final step is to write down each column in the order shown by the numbers of your key. So the one headed 1 goes first, followed by the one headed 2 and so on until you have the full ciphertext of your coded message.

```
IITEU CETHN GOTCS INHEI BIEND PSNDS
IOIGU SFLBD HOLH
```

Luke can decode this easily because the key tells him there are seven columns. Dividing the number of letters (44) by 7 tells him there are six full rows and a seventh row with only two letters. So he can draw the right size grid and use the key to help him write the letters in the correct columns. Then he can read your message by looking along the rows.

How to crack the code
Tibbs thinks this method of juggling letters is a brilliant idea so he has used it to send a message to Captain Cryptic.

```
ENNAH NPEBB TROGT IGLSA EIHSI ETUNS
DDSSE TTISE EEKAB TIHON DOANE NB
```

Luke has cunningly managed to intercept it but he needs some help to crack the cipher. Luckily we already know one very useful fact about Tibbs: he always signs his name at the end of a message.

Great. Tibbs' stupidity helps us out once again! That gives us what all codebreakers need — a crib.

Now we know the last word of the plaintext is "Tibbs", we need to find the letters of his name in the ciphertext.

There are several possible choices for each letter. If we find the right ones and put them in order to spell *"Tibbs"*, the letters above them in the grid should also make sense. They may not spell a complete word but they should at least make part of two different words.

Because of the way the cipher works, the letter above T in the grid is the one to the left of T in the ciphertext. So we know that:

The letter above the T will be B, G, E or T
The letter above the I will be T, E or S
The letter above the first B will be E, B, A or N
The letter above the second B will be E, B, A or N
The letter above the S will be L, H, N, D, S or I

B G E OR T	T E OR S	E B A OR N	E B A OR N	L H N D S OR I
T	I	B	B	S

Hmmm. I've spotted beans and teens, and ge ban could fit too if the ge was the end of another word. Let's try beans first. If it doesn't work, we can go back and try one of the other solutions.

If *beans* is right, the five letters above it should also make sense.

The letter above B and T is B or A
The letter above E and I is A
The letter above A and B is K
The letter above N and B is E
The letter above S and S is D

So the grid looks like this:

B OR A	A	K	E	D
B	E	A	N	S
T	I	B	B	S

Fantastic. It spells BAKED which is just right to go with BEANS. It looks as if we've cracked the code and discovered that Tibbs only used five columns. So now we can fill in the rest of the letters and read the message.

```
   TH
EREIS
NOTHI
NGTOE
ATINT
HISDU
NGEON
PLEAS
ESEND
BAKED
BEANS
TIBBS
```

Tibbs made life easy for us by only using five columns. Our job would have been much harder if he had used a longer keyword.

Our grid has two spaces at the top, but Tibbs would have written his with the spaces at the bottom. Now we know his message, we can see that his columns looked like this.

```
THERE
ISNOT
HINGT
OEATI
NTHIS
DUNGE
ONPLE
ASESE
NDBAK
EDBEA
NSTIB
BS
```

You can use his grid to work out the number he used as his key. Then you'll be able to decipher any other message he sends using the same key and the same cipher.

Answer: Tibbs' key is 53124. He worked this out from the keyword TIBBS but you only need to know the number.

Spot the cipher

Real codebreakers use frequency analysis to help them spot which type of cipher has been used to create a secret message.

If the letter frequency is similar to normal writing, it's probably a transposition cipher because a transposition only moves the letters around. It doesn't change them so it doesn't change their frequency.

If the letter frequency is different from normal, it's probably a substitution cipher because a substitution changes the letters. This makes uncommon letters appear more often and is sometimes so obvious that good codebreakers can spot it without doing any actual counting.

The problem of the poem codes

In the Second World War, the British Special Operations Executive (known as SOE) sent secret agents into occupied Europe to help the local people fight the Nazis. The agents kept in touch with headquarters by radio, sending their reports in Morse Code. They knew their transmissions were often intercepted so they used a transposition cipher to keep their information secret.

To make sure nothing was written down for the enemy to capture, each agent memorized a poem to provide the key for his or her cipher. When they wanted to send a message, they chose any five words from the poem as their key. Because the poems were more than five words long, they had plenty of different keys to choose from.

The agent numbered the letters in those words in alphabetical order in exactly the same way you numbered your codeword, "cat food", on page 88. Then he or she used those numbers to transpose the message before sending it. The agent would put a special indicator code at the beginning of the ciphertext to tell the person decoding it which words from the poem were used as the key.

Practice makes perfect?

Imagine you are an agent with SOE about to be dropped by parachute into occupied France. You're sitting at a desk practising coding with your chosen poem, "Humpty Dumpty", and you've chosen the words *wall*, *fall*, *kings*, *horses* and *men*. The only sound in the room is the ticking clock but you still have to concentrate hard to number the letters correctly.

```
w  a  l  l      f  a  l  l      k  i  n  g  s
22 1  10 11     5  2  12 13     9  8  15 6  19

h  o  r  s  e  s      m  e  n
7  17 18 20 3  21     14 4  16
```

Now move on three months. Your cover's been blown so you're running for your life from the Gestapo. You haven't eaten or slept for 36 hours and you know you're about to be caught. But you have vital information about Nazi plans – information that no one else knows. You must try to get it through to headquarters before you are caught. If you succeed, hundreds of lives will be saved. If you fail, they will all die.

You crouch beside a candle in a cold, dark cellar. There is barely enough light to write by and your stomach is knotted with fear. You choose the words from your poem and start to number them as quickly as you can.

But at the same time, you're listening for feet on the stairs and your body is poised for instant flight. It's so hard to concentrate that it's easy to do something wrong. You might number the keywords wrongly, misspell words in your message, transpose the columns in the wrong order or write down the wrong indicator code.

That's what happened in real life. The agents were under such pressure that they often made mistakes. When that happened, their messages were incredibly difficult to decipher. Although the people trying to do so knew how the cipher worked, it sometimes took them thousands of attempts before they managed to work out what a miscoded message said.

When perfection isn't good

Leo Marks was a code expert at SOE headquarters who cracked the trickiest miscoded messages. He knew it was normal for SOE agents to make coding mistakes. In fact, it was so normal that he expected it.

That's why he became suspicious when he noticed none of the Dutch agents were making mistakes. Such perfection was so unlikely that he wondered if the agents had been captured and forced to send fake messages. If that was true, the messages would have been checked before they were sent and any mistakes put right.

Eventually Marks' suspicions turned out to be right. The Germans had taken over the entire Dutch operation. By keeping quiet about their success, they managed to feed false information to the British, capture new agents as soon as they arrived and even persuade SOE to supply them with equipment.

When fame is not a good idea

Mistakes weren't the only problem with the poem code. There was another snag that was very serious. If the enemy codebreakers managed to decipher the messages, they could work out the key. If the poem was famous, they might be able to work out which one it was. Then they would have completely cracked that agent's code and be able to decipher all her messages easily.

To fool the enemy codebreakers, Leo Marks and others at SOE wrote poems for the agents to use. No one else knew them so the codebreakers couldn't recognize them.

Eventually the agents were given pieces of silk printed with lines of numbers to use as keys. The agents only used each key once. Then they tore off the silk it was printed on and burned it. Even if one message was cracked, it didn't help the codebreakers crack any others because each message had a different key.

One-time keys like this are a great way to make life difficult for the codebreakers. But if you want to drive them really mad, read on and learn how to defeat their most important tool – frequency analysis.

Outwitting the Codebreakers

As soon as frequency analysis came on the scene, the codemakers started searching for ways to stop it working. Codebooks were one solution but, as we've already discovered, they have several snags. What the codemakers wanted to create was a cipher which defeated the analysts.

One possible technique is to have more than one symbol standing for the most commonly used letters. For instance, the most frequent letters in English are e, o, t and a, so Tibbs could add four numbers to the basic alphabet and come up with a cipher like this.

```
a b c d e f g h i j k l m n o p q r s t u v w x y z
T I B S U V W X Y Z 2 3 4 5 A C D E F G H J K L M N
O       P                   Q           R
```

This has two symbols, called *homophones*, standing for each of the four most frequent letters. So Tibbs could vary which ones he uses as he enciphers his message. That would upset the frequency analysis and also make it much harder to spot common words. For instance, "*the*" could be enciphered as GXU, GXP, RXU or RXP.

To make frequency analysis even harder, Tibbs could also insert other numbers in his message to act as nulls – symbols that don't mean anything. So "Dear Captain" might look like this:

plain	dea r c a pt ai n
cipher	SUT76D B8O9CG8TY765

This would upset the frequency count and make the code much harder to break. But the Captain will still be able to decipher the message easily if he knows he must ignore all the numbers greater than 5.

The other big problem
But if frequency analysis doesn't work, the codebreakers don't give up. They have other cunning tricks they can use.

The Cunning Codebreaker's Guide

Trick one
Search the ciphertext for two symbols that appear side by side more than once.

These symbols probably stand for letters which often go together. For instance, in English, they might mean *th*, *sh* or *ea* but they are unlikely to mean *nz* or *iu*.

Trick two
Look for matching pairs of symbols.

These probably stand for double letters in words. If they do, and the message is in English, XX might stand for *oo*, *tt*, *ll* or one of the other possible double-letter groups.

Nulls and homophones can make this type of analysis more difficult. But they can't remove the fundamental problem with any cipher which replaces the ordinary alphabet with just one cipher alphabet.

In code jargon these are called monoalphabetic substitutions, which is a real mouthful but sounds dead clever.

The problem is that, once the codebreakers have worked out the meaning of one letter in the ciphertext, they know it will mean the same everywhere else. So they can put that meaning in and use it to help them work out the rest of the cipher just as we did when we deciphered Tibbs' first message.

Alberti's brainwave

Codemakers battled with the weakness of monoalphabetic substitutions until a fifteenth-century code expert called Leon Battista Alberti had a brilliant idea. If the problem was caused by having only one cipher alphabet, the solution must be to have more than one and to switch from one to another as you encode your message.

This system is called a polyalphabetic substitution.

IT HAS NOTHING TO DO WITH PARROTS!

The simplest way to use Alberti's idea is to have two cipher alphabets.

```
Plain     a b c d e f g h i j k l m n o p q r s t u v w x y z
Cipher 1  L E O N P Q R S T U V W X Y Z A B C D F G H I J K M
Cipher 2  A L B E R T I J K M N O P Q S U V W X Y Z C D F G H
```

Suddenly the codebreakers' task has become much more difficult because each ciphertext letter has two possible meanings. So E could mean b or d and X could mean m or s. Adding a third cipher alphabet would add yet another possible meaning to each letter, so the more cipher alphabets there are, the harder the cipher will be to crack.

Of course, the person who is sent the message needs to know which cipher you have used to encode each letter. Otherwise they won't be able to work out what it says.

Vigenère's square

Other codemakers thought Alberti's idea was so good that they developed various ways to create the cipher alphabets and decide which one to use. One of the most famous methods was invented in the second half of the sixteenth century by a French code expert called Blaise de Vigenère. He used 26 cipher alphabets written in a square with the ordinary alphabet along the top and down the left-hand side like this:

```
   a b c d e f g h i j k l m n o p q r s t u v w x y z
A  B C D E F G H I J K L M N O P Q R S T U V W X Y Z A
B  C D E F G H I J K L M N O P Q R S T U V W X Y Z A B
C  D E F G H I J K L M N O P Q R S T U V W X Y Z A B C
D  E F G H I J K L M N O P Q R S T U V W X Y Z A B C D
E  F G H I J K L M N O P Q R S T U V W X Y Z A B C D E
F  G H I J K L M N O P Q R S T U V W X Y Z A B C D E F
G  H I J K L M N O P Q R S T U V W X Y Z A B C D E F G
H  I J K L M N O P Q R S T U V W X Y Z A B C D E F G H
I  J K L M N O P Q R S T U V W X Y Z A B C D E F G H I
J  K L M N O P Q R S T U V W X Y Z A B C D E F G H I J
K  L M N O P Q R S T U V W X Y Z A B C D E F G H I J K
L  M N O P Q R S T U V W X Y Z A B C D E F G H I J K L
M  N O P Q R S T U V W X Y Z A B C D E F G H I J K L M
N  O P Q R S T U V W X Y Z A B C D E F G H I J K L M N
O  P Q R S T U V W X Y Z A B C D E F G H I J K L M N O
P  Q R S T U V W X Y Z A B C D E F G H I J K L M N O P
Q  R S T U V W X Y Z A B C D E F G H I J K L M N O P Q
R  S T U V W X Y Z A B C D E F G H I J K L M N O P Q R
S  T U V W X Y Z A B C D E F G H I J K L M N O P Q R S
T  U V W X Y Z A B C D E F G H I J K L M N O P Q R S T
U  V W X Y Z A B C D E F G H I J K L M N O P Q R S T U
V  W X Y Z A B C D E F G H I J K L M N O P Q R S T U V
W  X Y Z A B C D E F G H I J K L M N O P Q R S T U V W
X  Y Z A B C D E F G H I J K L M N O P Q R S T U V W X
Y  Z A B C D E F G H I J K L M N O P Q R S T U V W X Y
Z  A B C D E F G H I J K L M N O P Q R S T U V W X Y Z
```

This version of Vigenère's square uses 26 Caesar shifts in order. More complicated ones rearrange the order or use other cipher alphabets.

Before you can use the square, you need to decide on a key. You and Luke have agreed that yours is CRACKING CODES, so you can use it to send him the following important message:

```
The captain plans to break into the
Tower of London tonight.
```

Your first step is to write your key over and over again along the top of your message like this.

```
CRA CKINGCO DESCR AC KINGC ODES CRA
The captain plans to break into the

CKING CO DESCRA CKINGCO
Tower of London tonight.
```

Now you can start using the square. For each letter in the plaintext, the letter above it tells you which cipher alphabet to use to encipher it.

The t at the start of the plaintext has a C above it, so find the cipher alphabet beside the C in the left-hand column. Now look along that row until you find the letter under the t in the top row. It's a W, so W is the first letter of your ciphertext.

The second letter in your message is h, and that has an R above it. So find the cipher alphabet labelled R and go along it to find the letter under the h in the top row. It's a Z, so the second letter of your ciphertext is Z.

It's a fairly slow process and, once again, it's a tricky one to do when you've got bullets whistling past your ears. But fortunately you haven't got that problem, so you can plod on and eventually send the following enciphered message to Luke.

```
WZFFL YHHLC TQTQK URMAS HNXRY HWZFW
ZFSYR UPTGG GOWZW WNKI
```

Did you spot the words SYRUP and MASH in the ciphertext? They don't mean anything. They are only there by pure chance.

Half an hour later, you receive Luke's reply.

```
ZWXLW UPLZP MYBQY GRCQW T
```

He's used exactly the same cipher, so, once again, you need to start by writing your key over and over again above the message.

```
CRACK INGCO DESCR ACKIN G
ZWXLW UPLZP MYBQY GRCQW T
```

Then you need to reverse the process Luke used to encode it. Because the first cipher letter is Z and the letter above it is C, look along the cipher alphabet labelled C until you find Z. Then go up that column to discover that the Z means w.

The second cipher letter is W and the letter above it is R, so go along the cipher alphabet labelled R until you find W. Then go up that column to discover that the W means e.

You plod on, deciphering letter after letter until you can finally read Luke's message.

We will be waiting for him.

The good news

The great thing about Vigenère's cipher is that it doesn't matter if your opponents capture the square itself. They still won't be able to decipher your messages unless they have the key.

The bad news

Very cunning codebreakers can sometimes work out a key if they have some good luck to get them started.

THE CUNNING KEY-CRACKING CODEBREAKER'S WISH LIST

1. LOADS OF CRIBS
Cribs are brilliant. If I know a word is in a message, I can try putting it in various places and work out possible parts of the key. If the key is short, I might find all of it. If the key is long, I might find enough to guess the whole thing.

2. TONS OF REPEATS
I get a big thrill when the same sequence of letters crops up more than once in the same message. They could be the same word or part of a word encoded with the same part of the key. If they are, I can work out how long the key might be.

3. MASSES OF MESSAGES ENCIPHERED WITH THE SAME KEY
I love having more than one message to work on at once. If I can find the same letter in the same place in both ciphertexts, I know they have been enciphered with the same piece of the key so they must stand for the same letter. It's even more fun if I find repeats and cribs too.

The key's the thing

If you want to stop anyone cracking your code, you need to use the best possible key.

Criminal Mastermind Detection Squad

Report on possible keys

CAT

Much too short and much too obvious. It only uses three of the possible 26 cipher alphabets in the Vigenère square and is likely to produce telltale repeated sequences of letters.

CRIMINAL MASTERMIND DETECTION SQUAD

Much better because it is longer. But it's very obvious, so a codebreaker who works out part of it could easily guess the rest.

HEY DIDDLE DIDDLE THE CAT AND THE FIDDLE THE COW JUMPED OVER THE MOON THE LITTLE DOG LAUGHED TO SEE SUCH FUN AND THE DISH RAN AWAY WITH THE SPOON

A huge improvement. This will be longer than many messages so it will encode those without any repeats, especially if you miss out the second diddle. Simple to remember, but because it's well known it could be guessed easily if part of it is worked out.

EOCIGYAOGRKXTNPIUOECFCPRGAOCJFIU
CDUOECFIORDIOAGIUXPCURCODTDICYUIR
ACGDIARGCIUCRKIYCDPRAYUCDRFIPECGF
RGDUCNDOEIJCFGGDURFRPUDFROFIPCN
UDFCFUCGDPURFPRFUCGDFFPFGFPFPYU
CGFIRFFPFPDCPJJOOEOTUILEWX

This is an excellent key. It's longer than most messages so it won't cause repeats and it's impossible to guess because the sequence of letters has no obvious pattern. Of course, you'd need to write it down because it's hard to remember, so you'd need to be careful it didn't fall into the wrong hands.

The unbreakable solution

The longer the key, the harder the Vigenère cipher is to crack. If you use a random sequence of letters longer than the original message, the only way to crack it is by comparing two or more messages encoded with the same key to look for repeats. So if you only use the key once, your message is completely uncrackable.

This kind of key is called a "one-time key" or "one-time pad" because you only use it once.

Secret agents take lists of one-time keys with them when they go on a mission, just as the SOE agents took their lists of keys written on silk into occupied Europe. Like them, the agents use a different key to encode each message they send, and when they have used a key they destroy it so it can't be used again or fall into the wrong hands. That makes sure there is no way the enemy can decipher their messages.

So what's the snag?

You may be wondering why this isn't the end of the book. It looks as if the codemakers have won. If they've invented an uncrackable code, the codebreakers may as well give up.

The problem is, no code is foolproof and there are always plenty of fools around to mess things up. With one-time keys, the most foolish thing of all is to use the same key twice. Sometimes that's a genuine mistake. Sometimes it's because a secret agent who doesn't understand how the system works decides to be economical.

THIS LIST OF KEYS WOULD LAST TWICE AS LONG IF I USED EACH ONE TWICE.

It's also difficult to create, print and distribute enough one-time keys for everyone who needs to send a secure message. An army would need thousands of keys every day and it would be hard work keeping track of who was using which ones. So one-time keys tend to be reserved for the most important messages, with other code systems used for the others.

The Secret Agent's Handbook

Assessment Test – Very Secret Level
Which of these actions should you take to make your secret messages hard to crack?

1. Use a well-known phrase as your key so it's easy to remember.
2. Take out the spaces between the words.
3. Avoid using words and phrases the codebreakers may expect to find.
4. Be careful to spell your plaintext message correctly before you encipher it.
5. Choose a very long key.
6. Keep your message as short as possible.
7. Add some extra letters or numbers which don't mean anything.
8. Always sign your message "secret agent" so the codebreakers can't use your name as a crib.
9. Never send a message unless it's absolutely essential.
10. If you have to send the same message twice with the same cipher, always make sure both versions are identical.

Answers:

1. No. A well-known phrase is also easy to guess.
2. Yes.
3. Yes.
4. No. It's a good idea to misspell words and put single letters instead of double ones, provided the meaning is still clear. That makes life harder for the codebreakers.
5. Yes.
6. Yes if you're using a code book or cipher. No if you are using a transposition. They work better with longer messages.
7. Yes.
8. No. It's never a good idea to use any word or phrase in the same place in all your messages.
9. No. If you do this, just sending a message will show the codebreakers that you have something important to say. In real life, armies send lots of dummy messages to make the number of messages every day much the same.
10. No. Sending exactly the same message twice is dangerous – even a slight mistake could give the codebreakers a way to crack your cipher. It's safer to rewrite the second message so it says the same thing in a completely different way.

A super way to fool the codebreakers

Even if you can't use a one-time pad, you can still make life hard for the codebreakers by encoding your messages twice.

- Start with your plaintext.
- Encode it with a code or cipher.
- Now take your ciphertext and use a different cipher to encode it again.

This super idea is called *superencipherment* and it makes it much harder to use cribs to crack a message.

WARNING!!

Be careful which ciphers you choose or your superencipherment may not be making the codebreaker's life as hard as you expect.

- One Caesar shift followed by another Caesar shift just gives you a different Caesar shift so it's easy to crack.
- Reversing the plaintext and then reversing it again gets you back where you started!

It's safer to use two completely different systems. For instance, you could use a code and then mix up the result with a transposition cipher.

Choosing the right code

You now know a dazzling selection of codes and ciphers which all have advantages and disadvantages. Simple ciphers are easy and quick to use but also easy to crack. Complex codes and polyalphabetic ciphers are harder to crack but more difficult to use. So it is important to know which to use when.

The Secret Agent's Handbook

Before we send you on a mission, we will give you a low-security, medium-security and high-security code. Please decide which to use by looking at how long your information needs to remain secret.

To test your ability to do this, please mark each of these messages as low, medium or high-security.

a) "Plane delivering new supplies next week."

b) "The name of our agent working within enemy headquarters is..."

c) "I am under attack and need help NOW."

d) "I'll be out for two hours. Please feed the cat."

Your answers should be:

a) Medium. This needs to stay secret until after the delivery but no harm will come if the enemy finds out about it later. You need a code or cipher that will take at least a week to crack but it doesn't need to be completely uncrackable. The exact choice will depend on how good you believe the enemy codebreakers to be.

b) High. This information must stay secret, preferably for ever. Use as secure a code as possible – maybe a Vigenère cipher with a one-time key followed by superencipherment with a transposition cipher.

c) Low. Although this is very important information, the people attacking you already know it. In this situation, you are likely to make mistakes with coding. For speed and safety, we recommend you send this in clear.

d) Low. This information will be out of date in three hours and is so unimportant that it hardly needs to be secret at all. You only need to keep it from prying eyes so a very simple substitution cipher will do the job.

MUNCH!
MUNCH!

Life's getting harder

Complicated transpositions, polyalphabetic substitutions and superencipherment are even harder to use than they are to say. They are extra difficult to manage when you're hiding in a ditch surrounded by the enemy or on a ship being attacked by a submarine. So it's not surprising that codemakers through the ages have developed machines to help create coded messages...

Machines that Keep Secrets

The first coding tool wasn't a machine in the normal sense of the word. It was just a wooden rod. It was called a scytale and was used by the Spartans in the fifth century BC.

The person sending the secret message wrapped a strip of parchment round and round the rod without overlapping it.

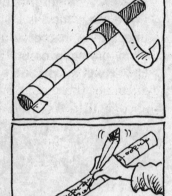

Then he wrote the message on it, writing along the rod, not along the parchment.

When the parchment was taken off again, all anyone could see on it was apparently random letters and squiggles. It didn't look like a secret message and it was easy to hide inside the messenger's belt. The person receiving it just had to wrap it round an identical scytale in order to read the words.

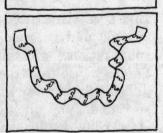

You can still send messages by this method today using a broom handle or a tube of sweets as your scytale. Just make sure that the person to whom you send the message has one of exactly the same diameter.

Cipher discs

The first real cipher machine was invented by the fifteenth-century codemaker we met in the last chapter, Leon Alberti. He was the first person to think of using more than one cipher alphabet and he was also the first person to develop a gadget to make using them easier.

Alberti's cipher disc was made from two copper discs, one smaller than the other. These were fastened together at their centres so the smaller disc could turn. Around the edge of the large disc were the letters of the plaintext alphabet while the symbols of the cipher alphabet were written round the edge of the small disc.

Alberti wrote in Latin so he only had 24 letters in his alphabet. This one has 26 so it can be used for messages in English.

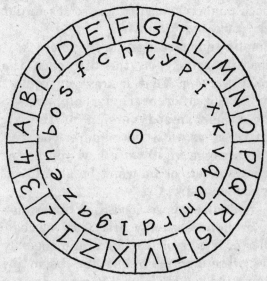

To send a secret message to Luke, you turn the small disc to a prearranged starting position so each plaintext letter on the large disc lines up with its cipher equivalent on the large disc.

If you like, you can use that one setting to encipher your entire message. As you've used the same cipher alphabet for the whole thing, it's really a monoalphabetic substitution so it's in danger of attack by frequency analysis.

To make your message harder to crack, you can change the setting on the disc each time you encipher a letter. That means you could use as many as 26 different cipher alphabets, so it's really a mechanized version of the Vigenère square. Just as with the square, you and Luke need to arrange in advance how you are going to switch alphabets or he won't be able to work out what you've said.

Alberti's idea was so good that cipher discs were used for hundreds of years. They varied in the number of letters on the discs and the way those letters were arranged but the basic principle remained the same. They all had two discs.

From discs to wheels

A coding gadget developed by Thomas Jefferson in the 1790s had 26 discs. It was called a cipher wheel and worked in a completely different way. The discs were made of wood and had a hole in the middle so they could be threaded on a metal bar. Each disc had the 26 letters of the alphabet written round its rim but each disc had the letters in a different order.

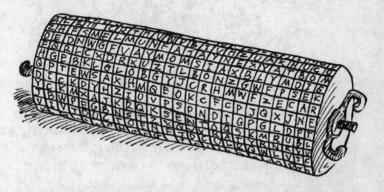

To send a message to Luke, you swivel the discs round to make the letters in one line spell out what you want to say, in much the same way as you would line up the numbers on a combination lock for your bike. Then you write down one of the other lines of letters – it's easiest to use the one directly above or below your words.

To decipher your message, Luke needs an identical gadget. He sets the discs to spell out your coded message and then looks for a corresponding line that make sense.

Cipher wheels like this are quick and easy to use, don't need batteries and are small enough to fit into a pocket. That makes them a good choice for troops on the move, although they are less suitable for spies because they are so incriminating.

The really great thing about cipher wheels is they use 26 different cipher alphabets so the resulting code is hard to crack, especially for short messages. To make life even harder for the codebreakers, the discs can be rearranged into a different order for each message.

Power on

The arrival of electricity allowed inventors to develop an electrical version of a cipher disc called a rotor. This is a disc-shaped gadget with 26 electrical contact points on each face. Each contact is joined to one on the other face by a wire.

To see how it works, you need to connect the rotor to a keyboard, a display panel and a battery. When you type a plaintext letter on the keyboard, an electric current flows through the contact point for that letter. From there, it goes through the wiring on the rotor to another contact point where it lights up the corresponding cipher letter on the display.

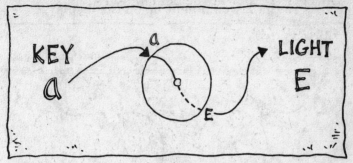

If you turn the rotor to a different position, you change the way the contacts line up with the keyboard. So typing the same plaintext letter produces a different cipher letter.

This looks clever and gives you 26 different cipher alphabets. But one rotor on its own only does the same as Alberti's cipher disc. In fact, it's not as good because it doesn't work if the battery goes flat.

HE'S NICKING MY BATTERIES!

If you add a second rotor with different wiring, the situation improves dramatically. As before, electricity flows through the first rotor to encipher your plaintext letter. But then the electricity flows through the second rotor to produce a different cipher letter which shows on the display. For instance, if you pressed a, the first rotor might change the a to E and the second might change the E to X so the X would light up on the display..

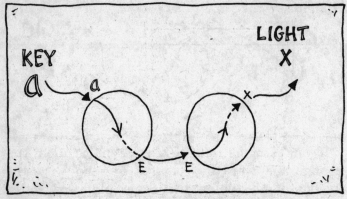

That might not sound very exciting but it makes codemakers jump up and down with joy. That's because they know that any of the 26 cipher alphabets on the first rotor can combine with any of the other 26 on the second rotor. So joining the two rotors together gives them an amazing 26 x 26= 676 possible cipher alphabets.

If your brain isn't aching too much already, try adding a third rotor. Now if you press a on the keyboard, the first rotor might change a to H, the second might change that H to G and the third might change that G to S so the S lights up on the display.

On its own, the third rotor would give you another 26 cipher alphabets. Now it's joined to the other two, each of those 26 can combine with any of the 676 cipher alphabets from the first two rotors. So adding the third rotor gives you a staggering 26 x 26 x 26 cipher alphabets. That's 17,576 possibilities and a real headache for the codebreakers.

The secret of Enigma

Three rotors working together like this were at the heart of the most famous code machine ever made – Enigma.

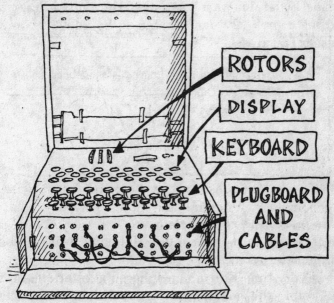

ROTORS

DISPLAY

KEYBOARD

PLUGBOARD AND CABLES

In front of the rotors was a display showing every letter of the alphabet and in front of the display was the keyboard. This had mechanical keys so you had to press them much harder than we now have to press computer keys. When you pressed a letter on the keyboard, a light bulb lit up a different letter on the display. This was the one you had to use in your coded message. But you had to look carefully because the light only lit up for a short time. That's why the Enigma machine was often worked by two people at once – one to press the keys and the other to write down the letters shown on the display.

The Enigma machine was the brainchild of a German engineer called Arthur Scherbius who first showed it to the world in 1923. Although the three rotors working together produced a really difficult code, Scherbius wasn't satisfied. He wanted Enigma to be completely uncrackable so he added several other features...

Be prepared for brain ache. Enigma is mind-bogglingly difficult to understand.

He made the rotors revolve.

The rotors turned in much the same way as the milometer on a car.

- Every time Enigma enciphered a letter, the first rotor (the one on the right) clicked round one position.
- When the first rotor had clicked through all 26 positions, it was back where it started and the second rotor clicked round one position.
- When the second rotor had clicked through all 26 positions, it was back where it started and the third rotor turned round one position.

This meant that each letter in your message was encoded with a different cipher alphabet. The alphabets didn't repeat unless your message was more than 17,576 letters long, which was very, very unlikely.

He made the rotors interchangeable.

You could take the rotor wheels out and put them back in any order. As each rotor had different wiring, the different arrangements produced different ciphers. There were six ways to arrange the three rotors so the codebreakers were faced with 6x17576 possible cipher alphabets.

That's 105,456. Is your brain aching yet?

He added a plugboard at the front of the machine.

This had a hole for each letter of the alphabet. If you connected two of the holes with a cable, those two letters swapped over. Suppose you joined G to M. Then, if you pressed G, the electricity would go to the contact on the first rotor for M.

There were six cables on the first Enigma machines so six pairs of letters were switched round. There are more than 100,000,000,000 different ways of choosing those six pairs from the 26 letters of the alphabet, so the combination of the plugboard with the rotors made the codebreakers' task enormously difficult.

He added a reflector.

After the electric current had gone through all three rotors, it didn't go straight to the display. Instead it went through another piece of wiring called a reflector that sent it back through all three rotors again. The system was carefully organized so the electricity always went back along a different route. This meant that if Enigma enciphered a as U, then, with exactly the same rotor positions, it enciphered u as A.

The good news for codemakers – This meant Enigma could be used to decode as well as encode. If you used the same starting set-up, you could type in the coded message and write down the plaintext from the display.

The good news for codemakers – The way the reflector system worked made it impossible for any letter ever to be encoded as itself. So a never became A, b never became B and so on. At first glance, this may not seem very important, but it was. It proved to be Enigma's fatal flaw.

Enigma catches on

The Germans knew that all their codes had been cracked during the First World War. After the war was over, they needed a new system and Enigma looked like the perfect solution. They bought thousands of the machines because they were sure they would let them send messages no one else could read.

126

At first they were right. When they first started using Enigma in 1926, the other countries could still intercept the German messages but they couldn't find out what they said.

This particularly worried the people of Poland because they feared Germany might invade. They needed to know what the Germans were saying so a group of extremely clever Polish codebreakers set out to crack Enigma.

The first breakthrough
As often happens, the codebreakers were helped by someone breaking the rules.

A German who was short of money sold some stolen papers about Enigma to the French, who passed them on to the Poles.

Those papers were just what the codebreakers needed. They contained vital information on how Enigma worked. Using that and some incredibly clever mathematics, the Poles worked out how the rotors were wired.

They still needed to know the order of the rotors as well as the settings for the rotors and plugs at the start of the message. To work those out, they used more clever maths to help them build a machine called a Bomba which could test the different rotor positions very quickly.

WE'VE CRACKED ENIGMA! WE'VE CRACKED ENIGMA!

NOW WE CAN READ ALL THE GERMAN MESSAGES!

But in December 1938, their methods stopped working. The Germans had added another two rotors to Enigma. There were still only three in the machine itself but these could be any three of the five available. That meant they had a choice of five rotors for the first position, a choice of four for the second and a choice of three for the third. So instead of being six possible arrangements for the rotors, there were 5x4x3 = 60 possibilities. The Bomba couldn't solve that problem and the Poles didn't have time to find another solution. They knew their country would soon be invaded so they passed on everything they knew about Enigma to the British and French codebreakers.

Cracking Enigma again

The battle against Enigma moved to an English country estate called Bletchley Park. The codebreakers there included mathematicians, language experts, chess champions and crossword whizzes.

One of the cleverest mathematicians was Alan Turing. He developed a more advanced version of the Polish Bomba which could cope with the extra rotors.

The new Bombes, as they were called, were very big. Each one was as tall as a man and over two metres long. On the front of each one were rows of drums which turned to test the possible rotor settings.

THIS MUST OF COST A BOMB!

There was plenty of work for the new Bombes to do because the German army, navy and air force all used different settings for their Enigma machines and changed these settings every day. The noisy machines worked 24 hours a day, their drums clattering as they tested thousands of possible settings to see if they were the right ones.

Hunting cribs

Before a Bombe could start work, the codebreakers had to find a crib – a word or phrase they were sure was in the plaintext of a message. Then they had to find the equivalent piece of ciphertext.

This wasn't easy but they were helped by the Enigma machine itself. Its fatal flaw meant no letter could be encrypted as itself. So the codebreakers could put the plaintext of the crib above a possible piece of ciphertext and see if any of the letters matched. If they did, they knew that wasn't the right place, so they tried again elsewhere.

To see how the system worked, imagine the crib is Morgen, the German word for morning, and the unbelievably short message is APMRSNGOFHEY. To find where the crib belongs, you put it above the ciphertext like this.

```
m o r g e n
A P M R S N G O F E H E Y
```

The two Ns match. That means this isn't the right place so move the crib along one place and try again.

```
m o r g e n
A P M R S N G O F E H E Y
```

This time the Rs match so it's still the wrong place. At this point, you may fancy giving up but the codebreakers at Bletchley Park kept going, trying one position after another.

In this fake message, there is only one piece of ciphertext that can be the crib – SNGOFE. But in real life, the Bletchley codebreakers often found more than one possible position for the crib. That meant there were more possibilities for the Bombes to test so it often took them a long time to find the right rotor settings.

How the Germans helped

Cracking the Enigma messages was a really tough job. But the Germans accidentally did some things which made life easier for the codebreakers.

They sent predictable messages at predictable times.

The weather report was the most useful one because it always contained words like *wetter* (the German for weather) which acted as cribs. Messages that said "Nothing to report" (in German) were easy to spot too. One message like that could help the Bombes find the rotor settings for the whole day.

They sent the rotor settings twice.

Before the Enigma operator sent a message, he had to set the rotors in their starting position. He chose this himself, clicking them round until his three chosen letters showed on the machine.

To let the people at the other end know his settings, he sent those three letters at the beginning of his message, encoded with the standard settings for the day. Then, to be absolutely sure, he sent those same three letters again.

GREAT IDEA! IT MAKES SURE THEY GET THEM RIGHT.

Wrong! Although it looked like extra security, it was a really bad idea. It meant each message started with a repeat, and that repeated pattern helped the codebreakers crack the code.

They made mistakes.

Sending coded messages was a boring occupation. It was tempting to break the rules to make life easier and it was easy to make mistakes.

One operator was so bored that he sent a test message consisting of nothing but Ls just because it was easy to type. The codebreakers spotted what he had done because Enigma's fatal flaw meant there were no Ls at all in the 300 letters of the ciphertext. That was so unlikely that they guessed what he had done. Of course, knowing the message didn't tell them anything but it helped them work out the Enigma settings for the day.

Another operator often chose his girlfriend's initials as his three-letter code group. By not using a different three letters each time, he made it easier for the codebreakers to crack his messages.

Submarine secrecy

Even the codebreakers at Bletchley Park found it hard to crack the messages to and from German submarines. The Enigma operators were careful to make sure there were very few cribs and, to make matters worse, the Enigma machines on the submarines had eight rotors to choose from instead of the usual five.

So, for the first rotor they had a choice of eight. For the second they had a choice of seven, and for the third they had a choice of six. That meant there were 8x7x6 = 336 different combinations of three rotors.

AAAAAARRRGH!

If you think that sounds bad, then take a deep breath. Early in 1942, things got even worse. The submarines started using a new Enigma machine which used four rotors instead of three.

EVEN MORE AAARGHS! THE BOMBES CAN ONLY COPE WITH THREE!

The codebreakers needed some help. Luckily they got it from brave sailors who risked, and sometimes lost, their lives recovering lists of rotor settings, codebooks and other information from damaged German submarines.

October 1942

Last week the British destroyer HMS Petard attacked a submerged submarine and damaged it severely. The submarine, U559, surfaced and its crew abandoned ship.

Three seamen, Tony Fasson, Colin Grazier and Tommy Brown, volunteered to fetch top-secret information from the stricken submarine. This was a highly dangerous task and sadly both Fasson and Grazier died when the U559 sank suddenly with them inside.

Brown managed to jump clear and was saved. So were the vitally important items they had already rescued from the submarine.

It has now come to our attention that Tommy Brown is only 16 years old. He is too young to be fighting for his country but had apparently lied about his age to get on board ship as a canteen assistant.

Could you be a codebreaker?

1. Do you think maths is...
a) great?
b) OK?
c) the most boring subject on earth?

2. Can you work out these three anagrams? (There's a hint at the bottom of page 138 if you need it.)

nonodl   srapi   tishwagonn

a) You did them without the hint.
b) You did them with the hint.
c) You couldn't do them at all.

3. When something you're doing doesn't work...
a) you try again and again until you get it right.
b) you try a few more times but give up if it still doesn't work.
c) you give up straight away.

4. Your favourite crosswords...
a) have clues involving anagrams.
b) have straightforward clues.
c) don't exist – you hate crosswords.

5. When you know a secret...

a) you don't tell anyone.
b) you only tell people you know can keep a secret.
c) you tell everyone.

6. If you were the best codebreaker in the world...
a) your success would be enough reward.
b) you would like your best friends to know.
c) you'd want to be famous.

7. How good are you at wordsearches?
a) You can do them easily.
b) You can do them but they take a long time.
c) You never manage to find all the words.

8. How many languages do you speak?
a) Two or more fluently.
b) Your own fluently and at least one other well enough to read some words.
c) Just your own language.

Answers:

1. There's plenty of maths in code breaking.

2. The ability to do anagrams is really useful if you're cracking transposition ciphers.

3. Cracking codes sometimes involves thousands of false starts so you need to be persistent.

4. Crossword-solving involves many of the same skills as code-cracking. Bletchley Park deliberately recruited crossword whizzes as codebreakers.

5. This is the most important question of all. Codebreakers must be able to keep secrets.

6. Because of the need for secrecy, codebreakers very rarely become famous during their own lifetimes.

7. It's really useful to be able to pick out words from a jumble of letters.

8. Many of the messages you are asked to decipher will have been written in a foreign language so it helps if you can speak at least one.

So the final result is:

Mainly **a**'s – You've got what it takes.

Mainly **b**'s – You could do it but might find it difficult unless you're working as part of a team.

Mainly **c**'s – Look for a different job.

HINT: All the anagrams are names of cities.

The Lorenz dilemma

The Enigma wasn't the only code machine the Germans used during the Second World War. They also had the Lorenz machine, which they used to send important messages between Hitler and his generals.

This was even harder to crack than Enigma because it had 12 rotors and worked in a different way. At first the Bletchley Park codebreakers made very little progress with the Lorenz machine. Then an operator made a mistake when he was asked to repeat a message he had already sent.

I CAN'T BE BOTHERED TO CHANGE THE SETTINGS SO I'LL USE THE SAME ONES. AND IT'S A REAL BORE TO TYPE IT ALL AGAIN SO I'LL SHORTEN SOME OF THE WORDS.

As a result, he sent two almost identical messages enciphered with exactly the same settings. That was just the help the codebreakers needed. After several months' hard work, they managed to puzzle out how the machine worked. But it was really difficult to work out the settings for each message and the Bombes couldn't help. They could only do the one task they had been built to tackle.

Before the war, Alan Turing had thought of a machine that could be told how to tackle different problems. The Bletchley codebreakers decided that was exactly what they needed to crack the Lorenz cipher, so an engineer called Tommy Flowers turned the idea into reality. He built Colossus – the world's first programmable electronic computer.

Colossus was ... er ... colossal. It took up a whole room and gave out so much heat that the operators used it to dry their washing.

THIS IS BLOOMIN' RIDICULOUS!

Instead of the silicon chip in a modern computer, Colossus had rack after rack of large glass valves. There was no keyboard or monitor. Information was put in via a long loop of paper tape punched with small holes.

Colossus had no memory at all and could do much less than the computers you use at school. But at the time it was built, its ability to process 5,000 characters a second was amazing. It made it possible to decipher the Lorenz messages before they went out of date.

Bletchley's secret war

If the Germans had known their codes had been broken, they would have changed them. So the codebreakers kept their work completely secret. They were so careful that they didn't even talk about their work to other people at Bletchley unless it was essential.

Did you know?
Some of the people at Bletchley were accused of cowardice because they appeared to have a cosy office job instead of fighting for their country. But they still didn't tell anyone what they were doing.

The British and Americans invented other reasons to explain why they knew the information they were finding in the decoded messages. They pretended they had networks of spies finding out the information and sent up spotter planes pretending to find submarines they already knew were there.

Sometimes the Germans were suspicious. But they were so confident about their code machines that they always decided they hadn't been cracked.

The secrecy surrounding Bletchley Park lasted long after the war was over. Papers were burnt and the Bombes and Colossus were destroyed. It wasn't until the 1970s that the true story became public knowledge. By then, computers were used all over the world and they had changed the way codes were made and used.

computer codes

Computers are great at boring, repetitive tasks like enciphering messages. They can use far more complicated systems than Enigma at lightning speed and without any mistakes. Of course, that perfection depends on the operator not making mistakes in typing in the message in the first place.

ONE OF THE OLDEST RULES OF COMPUTING IS "GARBAGE IN, GARBAGE OUT".

Modern secret agents don't need to encipher messages by hand. They can type them into a radio with a built-in computer programmed with all the ciphers and keys they need.

The computer encodes the messages and sends them at the prearranged time. The agent doesn't have to be nearby so isn't in danger if the transmission is traced. The computer can even make the message harder to intercept by using a system called frequency hopping. This sends it in short bursts on a prearranged succession of frequencies.

This doesn't mean the agents don't have to learn about codes. If the radio is lost or breaks down, they have to fall back on the old-fashioned methods until they get a new one.

THIS WILL NEVER BREAK DOWN... PHOOEY!

PING!

Computers as codebreakers

Computers have taken the slog out of codebreaking too. They are so powerful that they can analyse letter frequencies, look for repeating patterns and try thousands of possible keys at mind-boggling speed.

WORK, WORK, WORK...

TAP! TAP!

As a result, codebreakers have become so good at cracking codes that the codemakers have had to create even more complicated ones to try to foil them. These became extra-important when people discovered how to make computers talk to each other.

Cyber security

The arrival of the internet and email meant millions of messages were being sent each day which could easily be intercepted and read by the wrong people. Businesses, governments and people wanting to use credit cards online all needed a way to keep their information secret. So the codemakers developed special codes which only computers can use. To understand them, you first need to understand a little of how computers work.

The inside secret

Although we communicate with computers using words, deep inside their processors they only use numbers.

But their numbers don't look like the ones we use. Ours are decimal numbers based on the number 10, so the number 1111 stands for 1 thousand (10x10x10), 1 hundred (10x10), 1 ten and 1 unit.

Computers use numbers based on 2, so the number 1111 stands for 1 eight (2x2x2), 1 four (2x2), 1 two and 1 unit. These are called *binary numbers* and are made up from 0s and 1s.

Decimal number	Binary number	
1	1	1 unit
2	10	1 two and no units
3	11	1 two and 1 unit
4	100	1 four, no twos and no units
5	101	1 four, no twos and one unit
6	110	1 four, 1 two and no units
7	111	1 four, 1 two and 1 unit
8	1000	1 eight, no fours, no twos and no units
9	1001	1 eight, no fours, no twos and 1 unit
10	1010	1 eight, no fours, 1 two and no units

The computer uses a code called ASCII to turn letters and other symbols into numbers. Its name's pronounced *ass-key* and comes from the initials of American Standard Code for Information Interchange. It has different code numbers for the small letters and the capital letters.

Letter	Binary number
c	1100011
a	1100001
t	1110100
C	1000011
A	1000001
T	1010100

So the word "*cat*" becomes
1100011 1100001 1110100
and "*CAT*" becomes
1000011 1000001 1010100

If you leave out the spaces between the letters, "cat" just becomes one long string of 0s and 1s.
110001111000011110100

Each character is called a bit, so the string for "cat" is 21 bits long.

WHICH BIT AM I ?

Computer encryption

If you ask a computer to encrypt a message, it first turns it into a string of 0s and 1s. Then the encryption software changes and jumbles the bits in a far more complicated way than any human could manage.

Like the SOE agents with their poem codes, the exact way the computer enciphers the message depends on a key. But this key is written in binary numbers so it's another string of 0s and 1s. That same string lets another computer decipher the message.

The encryption software isn't secret. Some systems, like DES and IDEA, are used on computers all over the world. But the systems are so hard to crack that the only feasible way to decipher a secret message is by finding the right key.

If the key is only two bits long, it can only be 00, 01, 10 or 11.

EASY PEASY. MY COMPUTER WILL TAKE ALMOST NO TIME TO SEE WHICH ONE WORKS.

There are eight possibilities for him to try if the key has three bits, and 16 if the key has four bits. So the longer the key, the longer it takes to find it by trial and error. If it's really long, even a super-fast computer will take ages to find it.

DES was the first encryption system to be widely used. It uses a key 56 bits long, so there are 72,057,594,037,927,936 possibilities to choose from. When DES started in 1976, it would have taken even the most powerful computer so long to try them all that it was extremely unlikely anyone would crack the code.

But computers are constantly becoming more powerful. As the time they take to try keys becomes shorter and shorter, the encryption software has had to increase the length of its keys so there are far more possibilities to try. A more recent system called IDEA uses a key 128 bits long, so there are more than 300,000,000,000,000,000,000,000,000,000,000,000,000 different possibilities.

The problem with keys

DES, IDEA and all the other ciphers in this book so far are all symmetrical. That means the same key is used to encipher the message and to decipher it. The system sounds simple but it can cause problems.

If you want to send an encrypted message from your computer to Luke's, you've somehow got to make sure that he knows the key. If you meet regularly, you can tell him what it is. You won't give him a string of 0s and 1s. Instead you'll give him a password which his computer can turn into the key using the ASCII code.

Don't choose an obvious password someone could guess, like "password". It's safer to choose something weird like Gd3cmEG8.

If you can't meet, you'll have to send him the key. You could post it to him or send it by messenger but it might be lost or stolen on the way.

THANK YOU!

The only other solution is to send the key direct to his computer but you'd need to encrypt it to keep it secret. So you would need a key to encrypt it and you would need to tell Luke what the key was. Which brings you right back to where you started.

The open box mystery

The key problem set codemakers puzzling. Then, in 1976, Whitfield Diffie and Martin Hellman had a brilliant idea. Suppose there was a way of encrypting messages that had two different keys – one to encrypt the message and another to decrypt it.

Their idea works like this. First of all Luke sends you an open box. You put your message inside, snap the lid shut and spin the wheels on the combination lock. Then you send the locked box to Luke.

Both the box and the lock are impossible to break so your message is completely secure. You can't get at it and neither can the captain, even if he steals the box. Luke is the only person who knows how to open the box so he is the only person who can read the message.

Of course, the computer encryption system doesn't use real boxes. Instead Luke has a key for his cipher which he lets everyone know. He calls this his public key

If you want to send him a secret message, you encrypt it using that key.

But this encryption system isn't symmetrical like DES – it doesn't use the same key to decrypt messages as it does to encrypt them. So no one who intercepts your message can use Luke's public key to find out what it says. To do that, they would need his private key and he keeps that very, very secret.

Diffie and Hellman's idea was brilliant. It looked as if they had solved the great key problem. There was only one snag. To make it work, they needed an encryption system to act as the box – a system that used one key to encrypt the message and a different one to decrypt it. And nothing like that existed yet.

The prime solution
The solution was RSA – a system invented in 1977 by Ron Rivest, Adi Shamir and Leonard Adleman. It's based on prime numbers.

A prime number can only be divided by itself and 1.

To use this system,
1. Think of two prime numbers. These are your private key.
2. Now multiply your prime numbers together. The answer is your public key.

Multiplying prime numbers is what's called a one-way function. The multiplication is straightforward and you can use a calculator to help you. But, at the moment, there is no easy way to reverse the process to find the original numbers. The only way to do that is to try each prime number in turn to see if it divides into the public key.

Suppose Captain Cryptic knows your public key is 35. He's good at maths so he also knows the first prime numbers are 2, 3, 5, 7, 11 and 13.

2 DOESN'T DIVIDE EXACTLY INTO 35 AND NEITHER DOES 3. BUT 35 DIVIDED BY 5 IS 7. SO THE PRIMES I'M LOOKING FOR ARE 5 AND 7.

I AGREE.

That didn't take long, did it? And he didn't even use a computer. So 35 is definitely not a good choice.

To make the system secure, you need to use much bigger prime numbers. Choosing 23209 and 110503 would give you a public key of 2564664127, which is so large that even a computer would take a while to discover which two numbers you multiplied.

As computers become more powerful, they also become quicker at finding private keys. To make sure messages stay secure, encryption software uses enormous prime numbers to make it really difficult to find them by trial and error.

Of course, the system would collapse if someone discovered a quick and easy way to discover the prime numbers from the public key. But no one has yet, or, if they have, they are keeping very quiet about it.

Speeding up the process

The public/private key system works well but it has one snag. It's rather slow. As a result, it's mainly used to send the key for another method of encryption.

The system works like this:

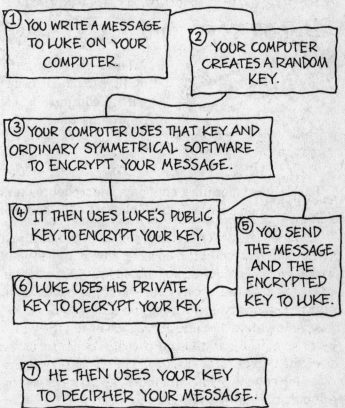

1. YOU WRITE A MESSAGE TO LUKE ON YOUR COMPUTER.

2. YOUR COMPUTER CREATES A RANDOM KEY.

3. YOUR COMPUTER USES THAT KEY AND ORDINARY SYMMETRICAL SOFTWARE TO ENCRYPT YOUR MESSAGE.

4. IT THEN USES LUKE'S PUBLIC KEY TO ENCRYPT YOUR KEY.

5. YOU SEND THE MESSAGE AND THE ENCRYPTED KEY TO LUKE.

6. LUKE USES HIS PRIVATE KEY TO DECRYPT YOUR KEY.

7. HE THEN USES YOUR KEY TO DECIPHER YOUR MESSAGE.

This system is very secure because you use a different key for every message. It isn't just used by secret agents. The same system keeps your mum's credit card details safe when she buys online.

Future perfect

Computer encryption is changing and improving all the time to keep pace with improvements in computers.

The codebreakers' ability to crack codes with computers is improving too.

That's good because one day the codebreakers may face their hardest challenge yet – a message from outer space.

Alien Encounters

By now, you've discovered that cracking codes depends on skill, perseverance and lucky breaks. It helps if you know:
- the language the message is written in
- who sent it
- what it might be about
- at least one of the words that might be in it.

So what about aliens?

Despite what you see on TV, it's highly unlikely that aliens will speak perfect English. That's hardly surprising, because millions of people on our own planet don't speak it either. So a message from outer space is going to be:
- in a language no one knows
- from a place no one knows
- written by creatures no one knows
- saying something no one knows.

That's going to make life difficult for the codebreakers. But before they can even start, they've got to have something to crack.

First find your message

Radio waves can travel through space, and aliens might use them to send messages. In the early twentieth century, people believed there was intelligent life on Mars so they scanned the skies for Martian transmissions.

At first they thought they had found some, but these turned out to be the natural radio noise that is always around in space, as well as interference from thunderstorms.

I'VE CRACKED IT! IT SAYS BANG, RUMBLE, RUMBLE!

Nowadays, radio telescopes scan the skies searching through that background noise for signals with regular patterns.

Next find a crib

If ever a message is found, the codebreakers' task could be nearly impossible. Just like the people who cracked hieroglyphs, they will need to find a crib.

Hopefully the aliens will have realized this and tried to make the task easier.

With a little careful thought, they should realize that, if we can receive radio signals, we must understand the science and maths that make them work. Perhaps they could somehow use that to help us understand what they are saying. Maybe something as simple as $1+1 = 2$ could help crack the alien code.

In the meantime
The code experts have plenty to do while they are waiting for that alien message to arrive. Computers haven't taken over the world of codes. They have just made it more complicated.

Sometimes the codebreakers have a breakthrough.

Sometimes the codemakers come up with a brilliant new idea.

The battle between the codemakers and the codebreakers will go on for ever. The current score is...

In the secret world of codes, no one knows for sure what's happening. But there's one thing we *can* be sure of. As long as there are secret messages, there will always be a need for cracking codes.

If you enjoyed *Cracking Codes*,
look out for *Spectacular Special Effects*,
by the same author